AF225457

The Cards You're Dealt

A Compassionate Grief Recovery Guide and Meditations for Healing After Loss

ERIN WEST

© Copyright Erin West 2021 - All rights reserved.

The content contained within this book may not be reproduced, duplicated or transmitted without direct written permission from the author or the publisher.

Under no circumstances will any blame or legal responsibility be held against the publisher, or author, for any damages, reparation, or monetary loss due to the information contained within this book, either directly or indirectly.

Legal Notice:

This book is copyright protected. It is only for personal use. You cannot amend, distribute, sell, use, quote or paraphrase any part, or the content within this book, without the consent of the author or publisher.

Disclaimer Notice:

Please note the information contained within this document is for educational and entertainment purposes only. All effort has been executed to present accurate, up to date, reliable, complete information. No warranties of any kind are declared or implied. Readers acknowledge that the author is not engaged in the rendering of legal, financial, medical or professional advice. The content within this book has been derived from various sources. Please consult a licensed professional before attempting any techniques outlined in this book.

By reading this document, the reader agrees that under no circumstances is the author responsible for any losses, direct or indirect, that are incurred as a result of the use of the information contained within this document, including, but not limited to, errors, omissions, or inaccuracies.

Dedication

For Gar Finn and Mia. My family sandwich.

Elva, my Earth Angel.

*Thank you for being a constant reminder to live my life
to the full every day. That love has no boundaries.*

May you be at peace now.

Table of Contents

A special free gift for you

Included with the purchase of this book is the Mind and Body Connection book. Through reading this book, you'll find out how you can take the necessary steps to help you reconnect your body and mind for life's challenges.

Click the link below and let us know which email address to deliver it to.

www.erinwestbooks.com

Introduction

This life will be good but not without heartbreaks. In death comes peace, but the pain is the cost of living, like love. That's how we know we're alive. Elena Gilbert – The Vampire Diaries

'Loss' is a term that we all are familiar with. No matter what part of the world we belong to or what religion, race, or ethnicity defines us, 'loss' is a common denominator. We all have stories that broke us, shaped us, and helped us to become stronger. We are survivors, and we deserve to know that there is a life waiting for us, wanting to be lived and cherished.

Grieving is a process that an individual goes through alone. Before I speak further, I want to highlight that there are no right or wrong ways to mourn or grieve. How one chooses to mourn can depend on various factors, including an individual's personality, faith, life experiences, and coping style.

Every hurting heart should know that healing happens slowly and gradually. You cannot expect the change to happen overnight. Before you listen to anyone's advice about how you are wasting your life grieving and mourning, you must know that no timetable is labeled normal for grieving. In some cases, people feel like themselves after months or even after some weeks, and in some cases, it can take several years for people to recover and learn how to deal with grief and sadness. Patience plays a role here, and healing demands going easy on one's self. It would be best if you let this process unfold naturally.

I am writing this book to communicate with all you survivors and brave souls who kept on going after your hearts were shattered and you lost strength. Through this book, I have tried to find a way to connect with you and let you know that we are all in this together.

Everyone told us that life would be tough, but no one told us how to deal with it when it hits us hard in the face or when we fall and end up more broken than ever. One thing that I learned over the course of time is that people use different coping mechanisms to deal with their grief, and sometimes, how they choose to cope with their pain and loss is not the ideal way. They develop a habit of returning to that behavior whenever they encounter a situation that triggers their anger and pain. Such bad habits can only cause further damage.

I have seen people who harmed themselves in the struggle to silence their chaotic thoughts and divert their minds so they don't think about the matter that needs to be addressed. I am no scholar or teacher; I am just a human who has gone through similar circumstances and learned to live with the cards I was dealt. I have been through hell. I fell, got back up, fell again, but still found the strength and courage to fight back and rise again.

I read this online:

"Life and death have been in love for longer than we have words to describe. Life sends countless gifts to death, and death keeps them forever."

It gave me chills. How can someone come up with such a creative way to describe the relationship between life and death? But it is what it is, and none of us can deny this fact. We can look at it as a love story, how one keeps on giving the other everything it has held dear. We humans are just the same, aren't we?

Before I move on, I would like to tell you that it is okay to hurt and feel extreme pain. We are capable of loving so much that it begins to hurt some days. You might have already heard these words from hundreds of people before me, but I will still say it anyway. Because the more you repeat it, the more it makes sense. It is okay to hurt and feel pain. It is completely fine not to feel like yourself for a while. It is okay to take a break and lie in your bed all day. It is okay not to smile or find the strength to interact with anybody.

No matter how big or small people call your loss, you must never feel embarrassed or ashamed about how you are dealing with it and how you feel about it. But you can adopt healthy ways to cope with your loss, no matter what it is that you're grieving for. It can be a human, an animal, a job, a relationship, anything. You can ease your pain and give yourself a healthy space to recover from your loss and come back to life stronger than before by finding new meaning and gradually moving on.

About the Author

My name is **Erin West**, and my book **The Cards You're Dealt** will help make your grieving easier and help you cope with whatever it is that's hurting you. In this book, I am going to share 52 guidelines and some relaxing meditations that will help you find the peace and comfort you have lost. I am not saying that it will make your pain disappear because that will never happen, but you will surely learn to accept the truth and learn to live with your reality just like I did. And that, my friend, is the best favor you could do for yourself.

I have had my fair share of pain and loss. It has made me the person I am today, and after all the pain and struggle, there was light at the end of the tunnel. Today, I am doing great. I was 19 when my father developed palate cancer. It came as a shock, and we were devastated. When I was 25, my mother developed breast cancer, and during the same year, my father was also diagnosed with a brain tumor. Little by little, my world started to fall apart. I was 28 when my father died, and while our family was still coping with the loss, my sister got breast cancer. After six years, she died. This meant that by the time I was 34, I had lost both my father and my sister. It was a lot to deal with, yet I held onto the hope of seeing better days. But my dark days were not over. When I was 42, I went bankrupt and lost my home. After a year, my mother developed motor neuron disease. She only survived for another year and died when I was 44.

My journey might not be as difficult as yours, but to me, I lost everything I used to call 'life.' My parents, sister, and home where we created countless memories to last a lifetime were taken away from me, and I couldn't do anything about it. It was like I was on a train that, at every stop, would ask me to leave something and move on with the remaining. I had nothing left, no hope to hold onto, an empty life. I dwelled in grief, and suddenly everything just felt like it was too much for me to handle.

But *The Cards You're Dealt* is not about my journey. It's about OUR journey towards healing and finding our way back to our lives. It is based on life lessons, support, and motivation to regain strength and look forward to the days to come. If you are on the same train, I am here to help. This book might seem like just another guide to dealing with grief and loss, but if it can play a part in helping you rebuild your broken self, I hope it does.

I know what losing feels like. I have seen my life drifting farther and farther away from me in the span of just a few years. If this has happened to you too, even if your loss is considered a "small" one and people tell you to be grateful for what you have because some people have it harder than you, I understand your pain. I understand where you are coming from. We humans tend to develop such strong connections in so little time. Sometimes, we make a friend in just a few days or we adopt a pet that we end up loving so much it leaves a hole in our hearts when we lose it. No one loss can be compared to another one.

I don't like it when people tell you that it was just a pet or only one friend and that you will find another one. No, we never do. The connections can never be replaced. Some of us might have lost a parent, a house, or a job that was necessary for living. Don't let anyone tell you that you should not be sad because you have it better than others. If you feel like you are hurting and need to cry and mourn the loss of something or someone, so be it. Because mourning is okay; giving yourself a break is okay. You can unplug yourself from your daily life whenever you feel like it. You have control over how you choose to deal with things. If life takes something away from you, let it go and focus on how to keep that connection alive in your heart forever.

This book will give you the necessary tools that you need to heal and feel comfortable in your skin again. You might feel like your world has already ended, but if you are still breathing, there is a lot more ahead for you, and you will need to recover from your loss to lead the life that you are meant to have.

A small effort can go a long way, and once you take the first step, you will find it easier to keep moving in the direction of recovery and peace. This lighthearted guidebook will help you come out of the dark and open up about your struggle and journey. I wish to help you perform some easy daily actions that will not only offer you peace but allow you to find inspiration and cope with your grief.

Make this guidebook a part of your journey and take a small step towards healing yourself, mending your heart, and finding the courage to be better. I wanted to find positivity when life messed things up for me. I wanted a miracle or a reassurance that things would work out in my favor and that I would live to see better days. Every time I tried or thought that I found help, it was a dead end. It is my desire that no one else goes through the same. Writing this book was a decision that I made after I re-collected the pieces of my broken heart, gave my tired soul the time to heal and recover, and got myself back to life. I need you to know, if I could do it, you can do it too, and no force can stop you if you make up your mind to begin the process of healing and trying to make your grieving more bearable.

This guide is not problem-specific. I have something for all of you. If you are a mom or dad trying to deal with all the parental responsibilities, if you lost a friend, sibling, parent, child, or pet, this guide is for you. I know the anxiety and fear of developing mental illness by thinking too much and worrying too much. I know the pressure to wake up every day and continue with your life because if you don't, you will lose everything, including your job or an important deal. You begin to suppress your feelings and your grief. You ignore your feelings for so long that you no longer find yourself able to open up to anyone or even to yourself.

Think of *The Cards You're Dealt* as your friend, a go-to guide that shows you the way to ease your suffering and look at life from a fresh and new perspective. We must move on and do what is necessary for leading a good life, one that makes us happier and more satisfied so that when we lay on our deathbed, we know we have lived fully without any regrets. I hope my efforts help you and that you find the courage to begin your healing by taking this first step of accepting the help you need.

Chapter 1: The First Step

"Though the destination is not yet clear, you can trust the promise of this opening; unfurl yourself into the grace of beginning, that is at one with your life's desire." – John O'Donohue, To Bless the Space Between Us: A Book of Blessings

Accepting the fact that you are in pain and hurting is a brave move. When you realize that losing something has put you in a situation where you no longer possess the power to undo what has been done, the best thing you can do is accept your reality.

Grieving is something that you cannot avoid. To make a fresh comeback, you need to collect all the broken pieces of yourself and stick them together. It will take time before you will feel better again. Your days will be filled with efforts to cope with your loss, but that is part of your healing. So don't stop until you do find ways to cope. I know that lots of people might have told you this before, and that's because it is true. Making peace with the truth that you now know is the only way to accept your state and make the process of grieving a little bit easier. It might sound cliché, and you might even say, "you make it sound so easy when it is the hardest thing to do." I get it. I have been there, and I know how awful it feels when everyone around you keeps telling you to let go but you want to hold on for a little longer.

That feeling of emptiness and void in your heart sucks. You are ready to trade anything to feel happy again and get back what is taken from you, but it is impossible. The person or thing is gone, leaving you feeling empty, and now you do not know where to begin collecting the strength you just lost.

Loss is not an easy thing to deal with, be it financial or physical. It affects your emotions, mental well-being, and even your physical health. You feel weak and down most of the time and develop conditions like loss of sleep and appetite, loss of interest in worldly things and a need to spend most of your time in bed.

It is completely human to feel like avoiding your pain would make it disappear or be less painful, but facing it can pave the way to finding comfort and regaining your lost hope and happiness. Life continues to move on, which is why we must engage ourselves positively and productively to heal the heart and regain composure in life. So, let's take the first step.

At first, we think we won't be able to cope with loss, but then slowly, we begin to learn how to live our lives with that feeling. We begin to deal with things gradually. If you avoid your feelings, they will reappear stronger than before. Whenever something triggers them, they will start to reappear and disturb your peace. When you make space to allow your mind and body to face sad and painful emotions, you become more resilient and develop your inner strength. I know the loss has turned your world upside down, but you must not let yourself slip away and allow the sadness to push you into a black hole that swallows you into thin air away from your life.

It is okay to cry your heart out alone or in front of your loved ones, but to let that loss and pain define you for the rest of your life is an injustice to you. Being a survivor, I can tell you that is not what your future self would want from you. There is a lot more that can be done. You can keep that connection alive. You can mourn and still go on with your life. It is possible. You can make it possible if you go a little easy on yourself.

When things started to fall apart for me, I panicked at first, but slowly it made sense to me. By the time I lost both my father and sister, I understood that there is nothing I could do to change their fate. However, I, too, am a human, and I kept on grieving. Bad things kept happening one by one; they taught me how lonely and depressed a person could become if they do not help themselves after a loss.

This is why I want to help you begin to start life again. I am not saying that you should force yourself out of bed the next day after someone in your family dies or after the loss of a pet or friend or after your breakup, or anything that has caused stress and put you in a situation where you are no longer in a healthy state of mind. Take your time. Go easy on yourself. Give yourself some space and mourn the loss that is affecting you so severely. But one day, we have to wake up, get out of bed, and go back to our normal routines. I know it is not as easy as it sounds, but it will eventually lead to healing.

If you can take one small first step, do one small thing that helps you get up and get back to your life, you will be on the road towards healing. The thing is, there is no roadmap. There is no 'right' first step. You are free to navigate this space where you allow yourself to heal however you like. You are in control. No one can tell you exactly where to begin because there is no real starting point. You can take the first step, any step, right from where you are at the moment. You can go whichever way you want. If you find comfort in finding any hobby that gives your mind peace, go with the flow and allow yourself to engage in that hobby. Or maybe take one small thing from this book and begin there, like practicing meditation or doing something special for yourself. Any small thing that can bring you comfort in the moment can be a start. Because healing is not an event, it is a process, and it takes time and willingness.

The decision to change your situation and keep that connection alive in your heart is a powerful one. There are thousands of books about grieving, truly amazing ones, that can help you choose your first step. Pick one of the books that talk about grieving, any one, and begin.

In the beginning, it can be all about just flipping pages and reading what resonates or finding quotes online about experiencing and dealing with loss and grief. I assure you that, if you keep trying, gradually you will find ways to recover and deal with your grief.

The simple guides and relaxing meditations in this book will help you once you are ready to cope with your pain and grief. I know that I cannot fix the loss nor make that pain go away, but I hope I can help you with the recovery process. Because I, too, was in the same boat a few years ago, and I know how miserable one can feel at times. How depression can hit you on a bright sunny morning and how a panic attack can make your nights lonelier. I only hope I can help you cope with the loss that turned your life upside down.

I hope this guide serves its purpose and helps you heal, and if someday you feel like you are losing it once again, you come back to it and find strength. I aim for *The Cards You're Dealt* to become the book that restores your energy whenever you feel drained emotionally, mentally, and physically.

When you feel lonely and experience social anxiety, I hope this book becomes your friend and gives you much-needed support and help. I know a human friend is always better to talk to, but when you feel like no one can understand your pain and grief, you will always find this guide by your side waiting to serve its purpose.

I am looking forward to helping you deal with your grief so you can allow your heart to heal. Everything that I have included in this book, I have practiced myself, so I can assure you that these guides and meditations are helpful. A tired soul and restless heart can find comfort reading The Cards You're Dealt.

Addressing Myths Before Proceeding

I'd like to first bring you some comfort by pointing out that there are several myths that people believe about grieving and dealing with pain. I want to address them here so that you know what is true and what is not. You don't have to believe whatever people tell you while you are mourning.

If people tell you that it will go away faster if you ignore your pain, do not listen to them because that is a lie. If you try to avoid your pain and mourning, you will only make it difficult for yourself because when you keep burying things that hurt you deep in your heart, you will end up hurting yourself. When you stop your pain from surfacing, it will harm you in the long run. Dealing with your pain actively is the best way to heal.

You might hear people telling you to stay strong whenever you face a loss. The fact is that feeling anxious, scared, lonely, upset, and frightened is completely normal. You do not have to suppress the pain or avoid crying just because you want to appear brave. Most of the time, the statement sounds something like, "You have to be bold and strong for your family." Please know that showing your feelings is natural, and it will not make you appear weaker. Pain makes you human.

"Not crying means you are in denial, or you don't feel the loss at all." This is yet another assumption that people tend to make if you are not too expressive about your feelings. The truth is that people who don't show their feelings feel the pain just like those who are more expressive. These people simply do not like opening up or expressing themselves in front of too many people.

If you hear someone saying that grieving should not last for more than a year, do not believe it because every person deals with their loss in their own way. There is no predefined period that you need to stick to. Your loss is your loss, and that is completely up to you how long you take to recover from it.

The most disturbing statement/myth that you will hear is, "'If you move on with your life, you have forgotten about your pain." It is a lie because no matter how far you go, if you experience loss in your life, you will always feel the absence of that connection in your heart. Losing an important person or thing in your life is not something you forget once you recover from the loss. You can stop mourning the loss, but you will never forget it. It will stay with you forever. The truth is that you learn to live with your new reality. As we move forward with our lives, the memories we carry with us from our loss can be significant in defining our life goals and influencing who we choose to become.

Different Forms of Grief

A major part of the recovery process is to understand what grief is, and that road begins by understanding the different forms of grief that exist.

There are two forms of grief that are widely accepted. These are integrated or abiding grief and acute grief. (Sahaja Online, n.d.)

Acute Grief

This form of grief appears in the beginning when you have just lost someone to death or have experienced any other kind of loss. This grief is painful, and you react in a way that may feel abnormal to you. Your emotions and behaviors appear to be very different from your usual self. You might look for your lost loved one in a crowd or see them in your dreams; you might even try to speak to them while looking at their pictures. During this form of grief, your mind is fully occupied with thoughts and memories of the lost beloved; therefore, your sleeping and eating routines experience severe disturbances, and you will have issues concentrating. Rest assured, these are all normal reactions. Even though you feel horrible, there is nothing wrong with you. It is part of the process of grieving.

Integrated or Abiding Grief

When you shift from acute grief to abiding grief in the first few months following the loss, your wounds start to heal, and you slowly find your way back to your normal life. You begin to accept your reality, and once again, you become happy and satisfied with your life. You engage and interact with people and in different day-to-day activities. Your grief is integrated, but that does not mean that you have stopped missing the person or thing or have forgotten about them. You will still experience feelings of longing and sadness, but these feelings become a part of you, and your losses are integrated into your memories. Those thoughts and memories are no longer constantly occupying your attention and keeping you uninterested in what is happening around you. Integrated grief is different from acute grief as it sets you free, and your feelings no longer consume your mind or disturb your regular activities.

Complicated Grief

It is a syndrome that can appear in about ten percent of grievers. It is the result of a failure to transition from acute to abiding grief. It can also be referred to as traumatic grief or unresolved grief and is linked with social and health functioning and substantial impairments.

If your grief is causing symptoms like depression and prolonged sleep, along with other physical symptoms, including weight loss, loss of appetite, and suicidal thoughts, you could be experiencing complicated grief, and should consult a doctor as soon as possible.

Sometimes, normal feelings of sadness associated with our grief can lead to some serious problems and depression. While normal sadness that is a part of our grief may become easier to deal with after months, depression is a mental health disorder that is completely different from any normal form of grief. It can appear at any time and any place in the aftermath of your loss and may require treatment.

Uncomplicated Grief

This process is referred to as an uncomplicated process of grieving, which is natural and is expected. In this form of grief, painful experiences usually intermingle with healthy and positive feelings, including happiness, peace, and joy. Even though the positive feelings sometimes elicit disturbing negative emotions like guilt and disloyalty, this is a normal part of the grieving process. If the griever continues to hold positive feelings for six months after a loss, it is linked to good outcomes in the long run.

Stages of Grief

Five Stages of Grief

The five stages of grief introduced by Elisabeth Kubler-Ross are:

- Denial: "This can't be happening to me."
- Anger: "Why is this happening? Who is to blame?"
- Bargaining: "Make this not happen, and in return, I will _____."
- Depression: "I'm too sad to do anything."
- Acceptance: "I'm at peace with what happened."

If you feel any of these emotions after a loss, know that there is nothing abnormal about your reaction and that you will heal once you are ready. Everyone might not go through all five stages of grief, and that is okay too. In contrast to a popular belief, it is not necessary to go through every stage to heal fully after a loss. In some cases, people heal and recover without going through any of these five stages. Other people might not even notice if they do go through these stages following a loss. Also, there is no specific order to these stages, so there's no need to worry about what stage you are in at the moment or what stage you should be in.

In fact, Kubler-Ross was not trying to fit our grief into a box by coming up with this concept of the five stages of grief. Before she died, in her last book, she said about these stages, "They were never meant to help tuck messy emotions into neat packages. They are responses to loss that many people have, but there is not a typical response to loss, as there is no typical loss. Our grieving is as individual as our lives." (Smith et al., 2020)

Common Symptoms of Grief

Losing someone or something dear to you will surely affect you completely. You experience symptoms related to grieving the loss. I want you to know that the things you experience in the early days of your grieving are normal. Even if you feel like you are losing your mind, know that it is normal to feel like this. You may also feel as if you are living a bad dream or may start questioning your spiritual and religious beliefs.

You may also feel anxious and numb. In some cases, people simply deny that a loss has happened even though they are fully aware of the truth. Some people also feel profound sadness, a universal sign that a person is grieving. You may feel empty and lonely and cry a lot without any reason. In short, you may become emotionally unstable.

Guilt can be another symptom of grieving. You may feel guilty about the things you didn't do or say while you had the time. Sometimes, if you feel relieved that a person's death eased their difficulty, you will feel guilty about feeling so even though you know it was better for them. You may also feel guilty for not being able to do enough to save them from dying.

In some cases, anger becomes a more prominent symptom of grieving. You may become aggressive and resentful. It usually happens when you lose a loved one; you become angry and mad at them for abandoning you and leaving you alone. You may also blame someone else for your loss in such a situation even though they had nothing to do with it.

Another common symptom is fear. When you lose someone or something, you develop fear triggered by this loss. You may feel anxious, insecure, and helpless. Panic attacks are also some common signs of fear and common symptoms of grieving. You may even start to worry about your own mortality if a loved one dies.

Apart from these emotional symptoms, there are some major physical symptoms of grieving, and they include:

- Nausea
- Lowered immunity
- Insomnia

- Fatigue
- Weight loss or weight gain
- Aches and pains (Smith et al., 2020)

How to Deal with Grief?

It is hard to take care of yourself after a major loss. However, this guide is going to give you some options, and believe me, these can help you change your life and your perspective on coping with your loss. Some of these guidelines might sound bizarre and funny, but remember, you should do stuff that makes you happy, comfortable, and relaxed when you are healing.

My life was never easy. I had to deal with losses that I never saw coming, but I had to become a brave soldier and fight when the time came. I intend to help you do the same because no one can stop or change the inevitable, but we can surely learn to accept the changes and cope with the losses.

To be honest, there is no predefined way to deal with grief and heal. We all have our coping mechanisms. Some people use humor, some use anger, and some just choose to dwell on their grief until they reach the point where they need help. No guidebook is magic. Grief is something that just disturbs you inside and out. You mourn a place, thing, or person after it has gone away. Grief hits in waves. One minute you are laughing out loud at a silly joke, and the next minute you are curled up in a ball crying your heart out on the sofa. So the only help we can offer ourselves is to allow the waves to come and to let our mind and body heal fully. You must start with learning to let go.

Dealing with grief is an important topic that very few people talk about. I wish not to be one of them. When I suffered, I realized how important it was for me to know how to deal with the losses that left me empty and led me astray. I realized that grief is not something that you feel for a day or two; it is a feeling, a phase, one that you have to go through in order to come out changed and well-prepared for the days to come.

After a major loss, a person must not make any big changes to their life immediately because it is not the time to deal with such matters that could lead to anxiety or further emotional instability. Making rash decisions is not a way to cope with your grief. Take your time and let things be. Just ensure you have everything under control until you are emotionally stable.

Chapter 2: Window Weather

"I feel that it is healthier to look out at the world through a window than through a mirror. Otherwise, all you see is yourself and whatever is behind you." – Bill Withers

There are days when you just want to sit with yourself and give yourself space to navigate through your grief or just sit calmly and let the peace sink in. Such days are helpful when it comes to realizing where you are in your life right now and whether you want to be in that spot. Moving on is never going to be easy after a loss. Grieving can last for days, weeks, or even years. Different days affect your mood wholly differently.

When the weather is dreary, and it's cold and dark outside, and all I want to do is stay warm and cozy wrapped up inside, looking out the window, my daughter and I will say, "It's a perfect day for window weather."

You do not need a bright sunny morning to feel fresh; similarly, you do not need a dark and cold night to cry. Every day is your day, and you can make it and plan it as you want. Everyone reacts differently after a loss. As we discussed earlier, it is okay to spend your days in bed if you need to. You can cope with your grief as you see fit. No one, not even I, can tell you how you are supposed to spend your days. When the weather is cold and all you want to do is wrap yourself up in a blanket, then you can do that and nobody has the right to tell you not to.

In fact, I suggest making such days window weather days. All you need is hot milk, tea, or your favorite coffee and a warm cozy blanket to sit by the window. Don't focus on one thing; let your mind wander. Think about whatever things your mind can recall. Remember the memories you hold dear, the good ones or the ones that make you cry because it is okay to cry your heart out on a window weather day. Don't pick just one day; pick any day and give it to yourself as me-time. Put yourself in charge of your thoughts and your heart. Decide what it is that you want to focus on.

Though there is not much that your body can find the strength to do, you can make small moves to make the situation better for yourself.

I prefer looking at the outside world and shutting down the voices in my mind. It helps to relax and enjoy some peaceful time as you see the sun setting, telling you there is another day to come. It gives hope, and one can realize how peacefully the sun lets go and allows the moon to take over the sky. It can teach us that even these celestial bodies are familiar with the art of letting go.

"How lucky I am to have something that makes saying goodbye so hard." – Winnie-the-Pooh

Here are some guidelines to help you as you sit by your window and watch nature:

Allow Yourself to Daydream

Almost all of us daydreamed when we were kids, but as we grew up, we were taught that daydreaming was a waste of time. However, when you are recovering from a loss and grieving, spending some time daydreaming could be just what you need. When you are having me-time, the best thing you can do for yourself is to let your mind wander without limiting your thinking.

Daydreaming allows us to let in all our far-flung or obscure thoughts and can make us feel ready to try any new scenario or solution that interests us, whether practical or emotional. Our cognitive dexterity is honed via daydreaming. What usually happens is that we take a complication and try to look at it from an entirely new angle. Also, it allows us to reflect on our overriding emotions and process them deeply on an extraordinary level.

Indulging in a fantasy that we wish would come true or in a scenario that is impossible amuses us and makes us feel better. Sometimes a little bit of wild imagination is all we need to relax and fully become ourselves.

If we think about it, some of the greatest inventions were created as a result of daydreaming. And not only inventions, but also powerful ideas, theories, and innovative creations. If you ever had a moment where you were able to figure out a problem while in the shower, you can surely relate to this. It has probably happened to all of us. We can't think of daydreaming as a shiftless indulgence; it is basically an essential part of the cerebral jackpot.

Daydreaming has a special neurological profile that paves the way for developing associations, random connections, or novel insight. When you indulge in daydreaming, you are putting your mental muscle into exercise; hence creative and critical thinking happens. In short, you sow the seed for your self-development, and sometimes you might end up finding a valuable solution to a challenge or an answer to a question. Therefore, giving yourself some time to daydream is essential, so turn those gadgets off and let your mind run free.

Hot Water Bottle - A Quick Fix

When sitting by the window in cold weather, trying to make sense of the things you have ignored for a long time or the things bothering you, don't forget to fill a hot water bottle and let it warm you up.

A hot water bottle is typically used to warm up the bed on colder days and can be used to soothe minor aches and pains. The sensation of a small amount of heat on specific areas of the body can be extremely comforting. A hot water bottle can help in many ways, such as:

- Relieving headaches
- Soothing backaches
- Easing stomach cramps
- Helping improve mood (Geddes, 2018)

Let the hot water do its job and warm you up when you are feeling upset or depressed. It actually helped me on days when I was not feeling like myself.

A Cup of Your Favorite Drink

Consuming your favorite food or drinks can help boost your mood. You can enjoy your drink and feel a sense of relaxation as you spend quality time with yourself.

An analysis that took place in 2016 and covered 11 observational studies conducted in China from 1980 to 2015 showed that caffeine helped reduce depression levels in individuals.

One more analysis that covered 12 studies observed the relationship between depression and caffeine. It looked at the data of 246,913 people, including 8,146 people who had depression. The study showed that the amount of caffeine present in coffee offers effective protection against depression. Moreover, it showed that drinking coffee was more effective than tea when it comes to reducing the risk of depression to some level.

A hot drink, even just water, can also help when you are feeling stressed. According to a study conducted in 2014, drinking hot water can help you reduce your stress levels and allow you to feel calmer and more relaxed. Aside from all other health benefits of drinking hot water, this one can aid in your grieving and recovery since it helps maintain relaxation levels.

There are several other benefits of drinking hot water; however, to me, this one appears to be one of the most important ones as it helps to calm you down. (Watson & Potter, 2020)

Put Your Feet Up

It may sound funny but believe me when I say that it works. Just like stretching can do a number on your stress levels, putting your feet up can help. Even if you feel nothing, do it for fun. After all, it is better than staying in bed all day.

Lie on the floor by the wall and slowly put both your feet up. Balance yourself against the wall and let them stay there for a few minutes. Consider it an exercise or a fun activity, whatever you like to name it. So the next time you feel anxious or upset, put your feet up. You will thank me later.

Use Your Favorite Cushion or Blanket

If you have a blanket or a cushion that is your favorite, keep it close to you. Let your favorite things comfort you while you grieve a loss. Using something that you hold a special place in your heart for can help you feel secure and calm. You deserve some pampering when your days are filled with sadness and discomfort. If you lost a loved one, you could use a soft object of theirs to feel like you still have a part of them near you. Sometimes having access to the belongings of a lost person can help you to feel at peace. If that helps you, snuggle up with their belongings and comfort yourself for as long as you want. Just sit by the window and breathe. Let the view calm you down and help you forget about what is troubling you, even if just for a while.

Music Relaxes the Soul

After a loss, one feels empty and feels like no one understands this feeling of loneliness. If you have just faced a huge loss and you are feeling hopeless, try listening to music. It can work as therapy to relax your mind. Music can heal you and silence the chaos in your mind. Music can help you silence those disturbing thoughts that make you cry whenever you think about that loss.

Losses like death are some of the biggest losses of all. They can change your life entirely, leaving you confused and messed up. No one likes to say goodbye to the people they love, but death is inevitable. When such a moment comes, try using music as your escape. Listening to pleasant music is soothing and offers health benefits as well

Play a song or two that reminds you of the person or thing you have lost and remember them as if you are trying to communicate with them. Music can help you relax your mind and body for a while so you can sleep better or improve your mood during the day, so you restore the energy whenever you feel exhausted.

Connect With Nature - Just Live!

You are going through a difficult phase, and all you need is some comfort and relaxation. You must not be worried about not making too much effort to change how you feel. It is okay to let yourself rest while you mourn. You lost something that meant a lot to you, a connection, a person, a thing that made you happy and was an important part of your life. You have every right to be upset. You are not overreacting.

Tell yourself that it is fair to be sad for a while as you sit by the window and watch nature. Do not worry about wasting your time and letting the days pass by without making a major effort. You are not in a race where you must keep running in order to win. Your life is a journey, and it includes lots of ups and downs. It is a bumpy road, and there are obstacles along the way. There will also be moments where you need to rest to restore your energy and keep moving. Give yourself that resting period.

Thank Your Feet For Carrying You

Sometimes, doing little things can make you feel good. Of course, life can be unfair at times, and you will fall without knowing how you will get back up.

You don't have to depend on anyone to tell you why you should be grateful after a loss because deep inside, you know you still have a life to live, things to do, adventures to embark on, and achievements to celebrate.

When you are ready to spend a window weather day, kick off your shoes and wriggle your toes. Stretch them out and say thanks to your feet, for they have been carrying you while you go through a dark phase. I can assure you; you will feel better.

Your body needs self-love the most, and only you can appreciate it for what it has done for you. Your feet have been doing a lot to support you. Even after you fall, your feet can get you back up after a little rest.

Give Yourself a Hug - Self-Compassion

Stretch your hands upwards and feel your upper body stretch, now wrap your arms around yourself in a hugging position and give thanks for your self-compassion.

Make self-compassion a part of your daily routine when you are mourning a loss. One easy way is to be kind to yourself and love yourself for the way you are, even when you are grieving. Wrap your arms around yourself and hug yourself. This may seem silly, but you will enjoy saying thanks to yourself for being so strong and brave.

Showing love to yourself will boost your mood and help you feel better about yourself.

On window weather days, make sure you do this and tell yourself that you are proud of this version of yourself, and that even though things are not working out in your favor right now, you are doing great.

Appreciate yourself for surviving after a great loss, and do not feel like your life has just lost its meaning. Assuming so will only bring down your morale and cause depression. Accepting that you are making progress every day is just another simple way of recovering from your grief.

So if you are depressed today, give yourself a warm hug and show yourself some love. Your body requires self-love in order to function, and your mind needs to be in your control if you want to heal and cope with your grief in time.

Deep Breathing

When you are mourning a loss, you feel hopeless and empty. Your life suddenly becomes too much to deal with, and you run out of energy. During this time, all you can do to help yourself is to show self-love and self-compassion. Little by little, you can tell yourself how you are making progress by waking up every day and engaging in small tasks like sleeping, eating, showering, etc. Such small tasks also count because they keep you healthy.

When things get too much to deal with, take three slow deep breaths and release gently. You would be surprised how much this can help keep you calm after a loss. Losing yourself into the void will take you further away from life. Slow and deep breathing is a simple and effective way to maintain your calm as you sit by the window and connect with nature.

Grieving affects several parts of our body, including how we breathe. You may sometimes find yourself holding your breath for too long without even realizing it and suddenly gasping in order to inhale. Focusing on your breathing pattern and adopting some effective breathing practices allow you to become mindful of your feelings and emotions. The better you know your thought patterns and understand how you are feeling and how your responses to the world affect your grief experience, the better control you will have on yourself. You will feel a sense of control and calm to help during your healing process.

Chapter 3: Let's Chat a Little - Friendship

Friends play an important role in your life. No matter what phase you are going through, your friends are the ones who stay beside you. Most of us have people we talk to when things are not going well. We have a strong connection with these people, and they are always there to listen and give us a shoulder to cry on. Friendships last forever, and the loss of a friend can be one of the biggest losses we face.

When mourning a loss, we can expect our friends to give us warmth and comfort. We look for our friends when things aren't alright, and when we need someone to listen to us and understand us. Friends help us to feel relaxed and loved. Their presence tells us that we are not alone in this world and that there are people who still care about us.

In our grief, friends are important because some losses like death can make us feel exposed and alone, and we end up feeling hopeless, empty, and vulnerable. We think we have no other companion or partner to share our grief with. Sometimes, when we lose a loved one or go through a breakup, we feel like we cannot become intimate with another person, or now we won't be able to connect with anyone at that same level.

Friendship allows us to develop a closeness and connection with others that helps remind us that being lonely is just a temporary state and that you can always find people who love you for who you are, and even in your grief, they will accept you.

In order to be mentally, emotionally, and physically healthy, one must have good friends. People who do not criticize you for how you react and feel but accept you with your flaws and understand where you are coming from whenever your life falls apart and you suddenly start losing yourself. Friends can indeed help you not to feel so lonely. These people give you the space you need while checking up on you when they know things are not going well. Their support can sometimes become your motivation and comfort. This is indeed a two-way relationship but one of the most beautiful ones. Because friends don't get mad at you or irritated by you when you cry over and over again about the same things or when you call them at 3:00 a.m. just to keep yourself from feeling lonely.

Friends are good for:

- Increasing your sense of purpose and belonging.
- Reducing your stress levels and boosting your happiness.
- Improving your self-worth and self-confidence.

The best part is that friends help you deal with traumas that can mess up your life, such as divorce, illness, death of a loved one, loss of a job, or any other sudden disturbing shift. They are best at encouraging you to change the habits that are unhealthy for you and improve your lifestyle so you can lead a better life. We also listen to our friends. Whether they are experts or not, we value what they say and we understand it.

With the help of your friends, you can reduce risks to your overall health when dealing with a loss. Adults who have good social support are at lower risk of major health problems such as depression, unhealthy Body Mass Index (BMI), and high blood pressure. According to some studies, adults who have a good social life have higher chances of living long lives as compared to those who have just a few connections. (Mayo Clinic Staff, 2019)

Most people want to know what a healthy number of friends is. The best answer I could give is that it is the quality that matters, not the quantity. If you have one or two friends who are there to help you out, comfort you, motivate you and love you for who you are, that's all you need. You do not need to have a large group of friends in order to feel happy and comforted. Though, if you have a large social circle and all your friends are supportive, you surely get the chance to be comforted and loved by many. If not, a friend or two is all you need to go through thick and thin with you.

Some people find it hard to maintain their friendships following a loss. Some prefer to stay in touch with just a friend or two because of their busy lives and priorities like working, taking care of children, etc. It is normal to grow apart because of certain changes in your life; however, you can still find a way to connect with friends or meet new people as you grow. The fun and enjoyment that friendships can offer are unique, and it is worth investing your time in building those connections with your friends.

You don't necessarily have to find yourself a large friend circle either because, as it turns out, joining support groups or online groups can also help you talk about your loss and open up about your feelings. You may find it hard to talk face to face with someone and express to them what you are going through; however, sitting behind the screen in a virtual group sometimes makes it easier for people to voice their thoughts and open up about how they are doing. After a loss, most people grow quieter, and they refrain from going out or meeting anyone because they just want to be on their own until they feel like themselves again. But this can slow down the healing process, as, without support from your loved ones, including family and friends, it can be challenging to accept the new reality and make peace with it. Let's open my box of memories and tell you a little something about how friendship helped me cope with my grief and ease a little of my pain.

Erin's Memories Box

I remember when my sister was brought home to die, and during those last ten days of palliative care, family and friends gathered to offer their love and support. When she died, it was, without doubt, the saddest day of my life. My sister was 37 years old. She had fought with every fiber of her being to survive and had left behind her husband and two very young children. There really were no words of comfort anyone could give me. One of the kindest gifts I received at that time was from one of my dearest friends. She sent me love every day through her cooking delivered in a heart-shaped dish. That was fifteen years ago, and I have never forgotten it.

You may not feel up to hanging out with friends right now, and that's okay. Here are some guides around friendship that can help you and others find a way to stay connected anyway.

Send a Message to Your Friend

You may not feel like talking but maybe you can send a quick text or even just an emoji to let your friends know you are okay or let them know you are thinking of them. It can help you maintain your relationship with them and at the same time express to them that they mean something to you.

There is nothing wrong with asking for help. You can always expect your friends to be your shoulder to cry on or just be there with you as you grieve the loss.

On the flip side of that, if your friend is mourning, you know them better than anyone else. You may know that they will act like they don't need your support, but as a friend, you know what they want and need. So even if they are asking you for space, give it to them, but find ways to show you still care. You can simply send them a message or just an emoji to tell them that you are there to talk whenever they are ready. I have learned that friendship is more like a vow, one that stays for as long as both parties are willing to keep it.

Being there for your friends is simply telling them they are not alone in this world. Even if family surrounds them, do not refrain from making your presence and support obvious. Maybe your support, words, and kind gestures can help them recover from their loss or at least comfort them through it.

Give Them a Call

Loneliness can do a number on your mood, so whenever you feel tired or life just seems too much, give your friend a call and talk to them about what is going on in your mind. Discussing your problem and your grief with another person who understands you and knows you fully can help to release stress.

Getting in touch with a friend or two in a time of grief is a great way to help yourself deal with grief. Having someone to check in with, someone to talk to, and someone to have next to you can make a lot of difference. It may be hard to remember to stay in touch with friends when you have so much on your mind and heart, so you may want to set up an automated reminder on your phone or another device. When you see the reminder, it may prompt you to get in touch with one of your friends, who may be able to offer you some much-needed support.

If you are not the one who is grieving, but have a friend who is, try and stay in contact with them. Put a reminder on your phone to text your friend every Sunday just to check up on them, and in doing so, they can check on you as well. It is a small but meaningful gesture and a way to be there for each other constantly. After a loss, everyone might be telling your friend to be brave and strong and all the other things that people say to try and offer comfort. But sometimes when a grieving person hears the same things over and over again, the words lose their meanings, which is why, as a friend, you must not do the same. If you keep talking about their loss and how sorry you are for them, they might have a harder time connecting with you in their grief even though they desperately need your support.

Try not to be too specific about your friend's feelings and emotions in your conversations. A random call for a little chit-chat can help them relax and can divert their minds for a while. If your friend is keeping their distance and you feel like they'll know you are trying to check up on them, talk about something related to you. Make it a question and ask for their advice or help. If being more obvious can help, go for it. Tell them straight away that you are going to stick around whether they like it or not.

Write to Them

If you are grieving and just haven't felt like talking, if you feel up to it, you could write your friend a note or a letter instead of calling them. It is completely fine if you cannot do a lot. A simple letter or note in which you can tell them what you are going through or how unfair your life has become will be enough to open up about your grief.

Your friends cannot do much for you if you do not welcome them or their efforts.. Remember, it will only harm you if you shut yourself off and shut your emotions down completely. Writing to your friends can help them understand your situation so they can help accordingly.

Sometimes, new media cannot match that special feeling you get when someone sends a handwritten letter or note expressing their concerns for you. It surely feels unique and extraordinary. So, if your friend is grieving and has just faced a huge loss, write to them to show them they are important to you and you are concerned about their well-being.

A sad person tends to think more about how empty and unimportant their life has just become after they experience significant loss. It is important to show them they are wrong and that they just need to take their time to heal and recover so they can get back to their normal life in time.

Even if you are sure they already know, tell them that even though life is not going to be easy, you are always there to go through everything with them regardless of time or distance. Your efforts will not go in vain because when they are on the road to recovery, they will be thankful to you for not leaving their side.

One Call Goes a Long Way

Just as you can offer comfort to a friend who is grieving, if you are the one in pain, you can seek comfort from your friends in small ways. Try picking up the phone and giving one of your friends a call. Focus on purely enjoying their company. This will get you out of your worries for a while and allow your mind and body to relax. Try not to just sit alone in your room and dwell on your worries, thinking about all the things that are affected by your loss. Opening up about your feelings or connecting with a friend for a while without discussing your grief can offer some help. You can depend on your friends to give you solace when you just want to chit-chat about silly stuff or when you want to discuss important matters. These people know the art of making you smile or laugh, so yeah, they can be your go-to people when you want an escape for a little while.

One call and you will feel relaxed because that is what friends are for. Even if you guys don't talk about much and just discuss your daily routines, you may feel at peace by coming out of your bubble and interacting with the person who loves you unconditionally.

In order to find healing, you need to connect with other people, so you don't end up completely isolated.

Meet Up With Your Friends

Some people lock themselves up in their rooms and refrain from interacting with anyone, but a casual meeting with your friend is a simple way to relax your mind and spend some quality time with your friend. While it is perfectly okay to not feel like going out, know that your mental and physical health can take a toll if you keep yourself within four walls for too long.

When you are disturbed and coping with grief and loss, you can do your best to surround yourself with people who genuinely love you and care about you. There is no restriction on spending time alone, but having company can reduce your stress levels and negative thoughts.

After you have lost something valuable, although it may be hard, try not to confine yourself to your home. Instead, arrange a meetup with your friend and meet for a walk or coffee. It will help you feel fresh, and that is what your mind needs during your darkest phase. You may feel like you need to censor yourself or your emotions around your friends, but try to just be yourself and relax with your friends. After all, the time one spends with their friend is time well spent.

Connecting in the Time of Grief

If you are not ready to talk about it yet, figure out another way to connect with your friends so that you guys can still see each other and spend quality time together. It is for your own good. You do not have to force yourself to talk about your loss or your feelings. Try doing an activity together that doesn't require much talking, like watching a movie or seeing a play. It is better to just be with someone and live in the moment than staying at home and letting the negative thoughts mess up your mind and health.

Because after a loss, it is important to think about your physical and mental health. When you are affected, you need to get back on your feet, and the sooner you do so, the easier it will be to move forward. When days are dark and gloomy, catching up with a friend can help. If you haven't talked to them for a while, use it as a chance to catch up on what they have been up to. You both will surely have lots of stuff to discuss.

Plan Something Nice Together

If you are feeling alone, give your friend a call and schedule a meetup. The best thing would be to do something that you both like. Friends usually share interests, so think about something that you can do together. Enjoying some time doing the thing you are crazy about will be better for your mental as well as physical health. You can play golf, join a book club, paint together, or travel wherever you want with your friend. It won't hurt to leave behind all your worries for a while.

If you have a friend who is grieving, take the first step and ask them out. Plan something that you both are good at or love to do together. Your friend might not be able to take the lead, but you can do it for them. Help them heal by making the process easier for them.

Laugh, Cry, Heal Together

After a loss, it's not easy to share what you feel and what is going through your mind, but when you feel like talking or crying, try doing so with a friend. They are the people who will love you at all times. No matter how bad you cry, they won't judge you. They will comfort you better than anyone. If you don't feel like crying anymore, find a reason to laugh with them and forget about what has made you sad for a while. Tell them silly jokes or ask them to tell you silly jokes. Your friends surely know you inside out. They can spot what you are trying to hide behind your smile. You can heal by laughing and crying with your friends. Things will get better; you will get better.

Light a Candle, Be Grateful for Friends

You are blessed if you have friends. So, when the times get hard, and you do not know what to feel grateful for, think about your friends. Count them as one of your biggest blessings. Light a candle and say thanks for these wonderful friendships. Even if you have nothing left, having loyal friends can help you get past this phase and heal.

Doing so will make you feel better about yourself and about your life. Some losses can leave you feeling ungrateful and miserable; in such times, find a way to feel grateful and say thanks for those things, for they can become reasons to look forward to the coming days.

Lighting a candle can also help you remember the lost soul. It is a way to express that you love someone and you are honoring them. Whether you light a candle at home or a church or somewhere else, the meaning remains the same. This small gesture can be a life-changing statement for you as well as for others who support you during your grieving. Most people do not see how important this small gesture can be for your healing process.

Several religious beliefs say that lighting a candle does not mean that you only light a candle, and that is that. They believe this gesture holds meaning. If you place the candle in a church, you allow others to pray for your lost loved one. Moreover, virtual candles can allow you to express support to the people who are far away and mourning the loss of a loved one with you

For example, when you lose a family member, you might not have words to express your grief or your feelings; during that time, lighting a candle may help you feel connected to them so you can pay your respects and honor them.

I suggest you never overlook the change these small gestures can make. They hold great value, especially if you believe, as I do, that lighting a candle helps you feel closer to your lost person. Even though you cannot do much after someone you care about dies, you can light a candle and say a quick prayer. Tell them that you are thinking of them and sending them love and good thoughts.

Return the Kindness

Being kind to others through any act of kindness allows you to fill yourself up with all the positivity in the world. This positivity is nature's way of rewarding you for doing something good. So, when you have healed and recovered from your loss, return the kindness that your friends have shown to you. They have been there for you when you felt ungrateful and empty, and now that you are finally back to your normal life, tell them how lucky you are to find friends like them. Do not forget what others have done for you when you were feeling down. Try to return the kindness little by little. If you cannot do much, a little thank you call or message would go a long way.

Chapter 4: This is For You

"A feeling of pleasure or solace can be so hard to find when you are in the depths of your grief. Sometimes it's the little things that help get you through the day. You may think your comforts sound ridiculous to others, but there is nothing ridiculous about finding one little thing to help you feel good in the midst of pain and sorrow!"
Elizabeth Berrien, Creative Grieving: A Hip Chick's Path from Loss to Hope

When you face a loss, you are more likely to feel empty and unhappy. It is okay to give yourself some time to recover, but in the meantime, taking care of yourself is important. You may say, "Hey, I am eating, sleeping, and getting through the day, which is more than enough to expect from someone who is grieving." And, yes, it is true. It counts as progress, but it is also important to take care of your emotional, physical, and mental health.

In order to succeed in every aspect of your life, you need to be fit and healthy. Every other thing comes after your health. I will still say that you do not need to do a lot. You just need to work on yourself slowly, one step at a time, and you will gradually come back to your normal life. I am not saying you need to rush your recovery process because that is unfair even to yourself. But it is important to focus on yourself even when days are dark and gloomy.

You might not want to hear it, but I am going to say it anyway. Put yourself first even when you are grieving a loss. Be kind to yourself. It can sound funny, but pampering yourself while you are upset can actually make you feel good about yourself and boost your mood. Self-love is discussed so often, you may even be sick of hearing about it, but I cannot emphasize enough how important self-love is after you experience loss.

Taking care of yourself does not mean you are not being fair to the person or the connection you just lost. It just means that you respect and love yourself enough to prioritize your health so you do not lose yourself in the process of grieving for something that is already gone. There is a life ahead of you, and you are meant to live it. Prepare yourself to see the world again from a new perspective and learn to appreciate what you have because now you know how you can lose something in the blink of an eye. Do what is necessary so that you do not have any more regrets. Your mind and body need you in equal parts, and you must nourish them.

Every person grieves in his own unique way. The journey of grief to recovery is widely based on our individual personalities, but no matter how we decide to grieve the loss, self-care should be one thing that we do not ignore. Finding a solution and recovering can be easier if our minds and body are in a healthy state.

Rumi said, "The cure for pain is in the pain." So when you are hurting, try to address the issue. If you only circle around it, you will keep hurting yourself. Instead, move towards it slowly, go closer, and figure your way through it. Only by living through the pain will you know how to heal from it and recover your heart, mind, and body.

Here are some guides to help you focus on your overall health while you grieve the loss:

Watch What You Eat

If you have not been looking after your diet properly, begin today. Remove one troublemaker item from the cupboard. Sometimes, a loss can affect your diet, and you can adopt unhealthy eating habits that can lead to excessive weight gain or loss. The occasional comfort food is a good way to help you feel a lot better, but it is quite a fine line, and if you are not careful, you might end up making the situation worse by eating a lot of junk food.

If you have been eating irregularly and too much or too little that is harming your diet, make sure to fix that in time. Usually, people eat too much when they are depressed. If you are one of them, it is time to look after your diet and remove some unhealthy items from your shelves if possible.

It is a fact that unhealthy eating patterns can cause mood swings. Nutritional imbalances are the reason blood sugar fluctuations happen. It is through food that we consume the fuel our body and mind need to function properly.

If you miss a meal such as breakfast which is the most important one, it can affect your blood sugar levels, causing them to lower. It will make you tired and weak. Moreover, if you randomly decide to cut out entire food groups, reducing variety from your diet, you will face more difficulty obtaining the essential nutrients that your mind and body require. Low levels of iron, B vitamins, zinc, omega-3 fatty acids, vitamin D, and magnesium are linked to conditions like bad mood and lower energy levels.

Some people eat sweets and too many refined carbohydrates to make themselves feel better. However, if you consume high levels of refined carbohydrates, your blood sugar levels will surely increase, putting you at risk. You will feel low and out of energy all the time and will get easily irritated.

Diet and nutrition also play a vital role in keeping you mentally healthy. Research that links them together is growing at a fast pace. Recently, some evidence proved that what you eat will directly affect the prevention, management, and development of several mental health conditions, including anxiety disorders and depression.

Researchers are closely looking at how and why diet affects mental health. The ongoing studies explore the effects of diet on the gut microbiota, which are organisms that live in the intestinal tract; oxidative stress, which is another name for cellular damage; chronic inflammation; and neuroplasticity, which is the ability of a brain to modify function, wiring, and structure. (Magill, 2018).

Cook Something

If you eat a lot of takeout, prepare one home-cooked meal this week and try to incorporate it into your weekly meal plan. It is better that way. It will allow you to engage in a productive activity and to take a break from unhealthy food for one day. You may even enjoy cooking for yourself, and engaging yourself in the kitchen can help distract you from all the negative thoughts. Cooking can be even more fun if you try new ingredients and new recipes. So go ahead. Make your meal with all your favorite ingredients and spices, embark on an adventure and try some new things, and enjoy a healthy home-cooked meal every week.

Home-cooked meals are fresher and healthier. Think about your body for a while. Is it fair to your body if you keep feeding it takeout? Your body is moving you, taking you places, and giving you the strength you need to get past this phase of grief. It needs nourishment and pampering the most. So feed yourself some delicious home-cooked meals.

If you feel like it, you could even invite some friends over for a nice friendly meetup with good food. You don't have to hide in the dark when you are grieving. You can still enjoy the sun and cope with your grief. Remember, just the first step, and the rest will become much easier.

Develop a Routine

It is a common fact that grief can disturb your life. You no longer feel like being creative or sticking to a proper routine. However, living in chaos can affect your health and mess things up for you down the road. Just like kids have screen time, playtime, sleep time, and study time, we adults also need a schedule to perform efficiently, especially when grieving. We need to set a time frame to complete certain tasks and be patient with ourselves to follow that routine.

I suggest making a daily, weekly, and monthly routine. This has really helped me. For so long, I was going from pillar to post with no direction. When you are going through so much grief and sadness, a routine can really help you get through your days with less stress, so the simple day-to-day stuff does not overwhelm you. A routine can help you keep up with your daily tasks, so you don't feel the burden later of catching up on everything that has fallen behind.

A routine can help you outline important tasks daily, weekly, and monthly, and allow you to see progress at the end of the day, week, and month. In that way, you can see improvement in yourself, and the progress you make will give you pride. These little achievements are a great boost when you are feeling low and unmotivated. Of course, you won't get a hold of things at first. Remember, baby steps, baby steps, baby steps.

Give Peace to Your Mind

Constant worrying and thinking wears us out and tires our mind. When our thoughts are racing all day and even during the night, we toss and turn and rarely get the sleep we need. This needs fixing, and the best thing you can do is try out meditations and mindful practices. People use meditation to relax their minds and get the relief they want from their thoughts and the chaos building up in their heads. With a little practice, you can do wonders to quiet your mind with meditation. I will discuss some meditation and mindful practices later in this book.

Show Gratitude

In times of loss, we often might feel like we have nothing to be grateful for, but developing daily gratitude is very powerful and is a great mood booster. But how can you show gratitude when you are grieving? Your heart is heavy and full of pain. The key here is not to try to force a cheerful attitude upon yourself. It is just to meet yourself where you are and celebrate the little wins. Have you managed to do something today that was too much of a struggle on other days? It can be anything small like getting out of bed or taking a shower, getting dressed or putting shoes on. If taking a shower, for example, felt like an immense effort, but you did it anyway, congratulate yourself. Tell yourself you are grateful, even if only to yourself, that you managed that burdensome task. The idea is just to give your mind space to slowly allow some positive thoughts in, one day at a time, one step at a time, one thought at a time.

As tough as it is to even think about right now, a grateful attitude can actually help when times are hard. When you feel like your morale is down, and you don't have anything to feel blessed with, you can try to find even the smallest thing to be grateful for. Did someone show you a particular kindness that you especially appreciated during this time? Simply taking note of it in your mind counts as gratitude and is enough to help boost your mood. Feeling small bursts of gratitude can minimize the feeling of demoralization and give you the power to face your loss. It can bring power and hope, and can help you through tough times.

However, gratefulness is a choice that takes courage to be made. It is challenging to develop an attitude that does not get affected by any gains or losses, and that will come in time. Right now, small gratitudes can give us some perspective and prevent our emotions from completely overwhelming us during times of change.

Suffering and trials are ways through which our attitude is refined and gratefulness is deepened. Thanksgiving, a national American holiday, was created as a result of hard times, as the first one took place following a rough year and winter that took many pilgrims' lives. In 1863, it was declared a national holiday when the Civil War was ongoing, and later in the 1930's it was moved to the fourth Thursday in November every year, where it continues to be celebrated.

Any amount of gratitude can help you through hard times, just as it did for the pilgrims all those years ago, who were likely still mourning their losses when they chose to give thanks. Of course, no one is expecting you to throw a feast in celebration of your gratitude. Just one small thought at a time. Baby steps.

Keep a Journal

You might have heard a lot about keeping a journal to help you clear your mind and reflect on your feelings. Your journal is your personal diary, and only you know what's written inside. You can lock your memories, happy and sad moments, achievements, and losses inside, and whenever you feel like it, you can flip through the pages and relive those moments.

Keeping a journal is a useful habit. At the end of the day, you get to see what you have achieved so far, what you have lost. Questions like how much progress I made; how I changed; what made me sad, angry, happy, and upset; how I tackled a certain situation can be answered if you write daily entries in your journal.

Keeping a journal can also help you manage feelings of loneliness. It allows you to express yourself openly, release your thoughts, and free your mind from dark thoughts that demand to be released.

Journaling can help during those times when you are not feeling like meeting your friends. Instead, you can share your thoughts privately on the page in a way that harms no one, and you don't have to talk to someone face to face. If you want to stay in bed or in your room all day, you can still share whatever goes through your mind the whole day in your journal.

It is a healthy practice, and most successful people do this because it helps them highlight their achievements, losses, progress, and areas where they still need to improve. If you are not good at writing long paragraphs, you can begin by writing small phrases or even drawing pictures.

Benefits of Keeping a Journal

Recording things can also make you more mindful of what you are feeling. Certain individuals don't have the foggiest idea of what they feel until they record it. Articulating contemplations and feelings offers you a chance to take a step back and profoundly ponder, and maybe better comprehend, the feelings inside you. It's a technique for self-reflection that can uncover things you haven't deliberately considered.

If you are grieving a friend or family member, you can also make a journal to remember them. Write down your favorite memories of them and little details about them. Record their favorite songs, smells, foods, places. Write about how your loved one affected you and why. Write an account of your relationship with them and what they meant for your life, the great and the awful.

Often, directly after we lose a loved one, memories of them come flooding back to us, things we may not have thought about in years. Little things we remember about them are still fresh in our minds. Months or even years down the line, when we are missing our loved ones and looking to connect to them, we can revisit our journal and remember things that may have slipped our minds over the years.

I recently was reading through my journal, and came across a special memory that I hadn't thought about for a while.

My kids love fruit and, from the time they were young, my mom had always peeled and cut their apples for them. This was a very simple gesture but my kids loved when their grandmother did this so lovingly for them. A few days before my mom passed away I was out walking with my kids. I was explaining that their grandmother only had a few days to live and asked them what they would miss the most about her. My son turned to me sadly and said, "The way she cuts my apple."

Years later, when I was flipping through the pages in my journal, I was so grateful I had taken the time to write down this special memory. Now I will never forget walking with my children that day, remembering my mom with them, nor will I forget the way my mom made my son feel special by doing such a small loving thing for him, like cutting his apples. It really is the simple things in life.

During the days and weeks ahead, writing things like this down can be a source of tremendous comfort to you. You will also be comforted in the future when you see the memories your journal has allowed you to hold onto.

Aside from just memories, you can also write down any feelings you have related to your loved one. You could even write directly to them if you feel there are things you wish you could say to them.

A grief journal provides you a safe spot sans judgment to investigate your confused contemplations and sentiments, to recall your adored one and to record your continuous journey through your grief. It's consoling to think back and see exactly how far you've come from the very first moment. Now and then, you may feel like you aren't gaining any headway whatsoever, yet when you have something substantial to look back on, it's easier to see how far you've come.

There are no rules. This journal is for you, and you can use it in the manner in which you see fit. There might be days that you don't want to write. That is alright. You can likewise draw, shade, paint, stick, or make something different in its pages. It's altogether dependent upon you. It's your space.

Journaling can really improve your physical and emotional well-being. Articulating your thoughts and feelings helps you work through them so you can begin to heal. It helps you release bottled up feelings that you might not have even known you had. This can help quiet your mind and bring you peace.

Move Your Body

Exercise is the best way to keep your mind and body healthy. I cannot emphasize the benefits of exercise enough. It not only keeps you healthy and energetic but it can also keep your mind off of your negative thoughts. You feel less stressed when you are active throughout the day.

When you are grieving, engaging yourself in some kind of exercise is just like feeding yourself healthy food. Though it may not eliminate grief once and for all, it can play a vital role in helping you adapt to the loss you have just faced.

When you do any physical activity, your brain releases chemicals known as endorphins. These guys help us boost our mood and minimize discomfort. So if you can do even a little bit of exercise when you are grieving and feeling depressed, you may find that it helps you feel better.

A study conducted by the Black Dog Institute in 2017 found that exercising regularly, regardless of its intensity, prevents depression, and exercising for only one hour can do the job. (Smith, 2018)

When your mood is regulated through exercise, you feel full of energy and active. This can help you find the strength to take care of important daily tasks that you haven't found the motivation to do. Moving your body and doing any kind of exercise, whether it's walking, hiking, yoga, or even doing workout videos in your living room, can help you make it through the days and aid in the healing process.

Exercise to Deal with Grief

Exercise can also help create that subtle sensation of satisfaction. During exercise, a protein that lives within nerve cells is produced. It is known as BDNF. When you exercise, it raises your pulse and BDNF is delivered. This protein aids in the functioning of neurons and allows the growth of new neurons. As a result, our brains work better.

BDNF has been associated with improved memory. It also works as a natural antidepressant and battles uneasiness.

Furthermore, exercise allows your body to produce the feel-good hormone commonly known as dopamine. When you hit the gym, take a walk, or even work out at home, this hormone is released by your body. As soon as you are done working out, you will feel better, happier, and more in control of your emotions.

Exercise helps you regain composure, and it provides great health benefits as well. Whether you are stressed, depressed, anxious, or are experiencing fluctuating blood pressure, a little exercise can go a long way towards helping you feel better. It is comforting, and it is just what you might need to step out of the negativity.

Running, if you are up for it, is a great mood booster as well and an activity that can be done alone. You don't need anyone to assist you while you do it. A solo activity like running keeps away the pressure of competition and fear of judgment because no one is there to judge you or criticize you. It allows you to hold your bag of thoughts and sort them out while you move. If you can't or don't want to run, even brisk walking silently or while listening to music can help shut down some of the chaos messing with your mind.

The departure of a friend or family member is a breaking experience. It will affect our mind, body, and soul. We can immediately feel the effect it has on our emotions, but we may not even realize when the sorrow of losing somebody also begins to affect our body.

When we are under the stress of grieving, our body starts to create increased levels of cortisone, which can make us more susceptible to sickness. It's not unusual to experience minor diseases and ailments during seasons of loss. Absence of sleep, loss of appetite, and an overall feeling of sickness are regular reactions to sorrow and grief, and the physical effects of exercise discussed above can help alleviate some of these symptoms. Getting up, getting out there and moving your body is probably one of the toughest things to begin when you are feeling down, but it can also be one of the most beneficial to the recovery process.

Get Help from a Grief Counselor or Therapist

Sometimes, we find it hard to communicate with our friends about our grief and the loss we have suffered. We feel like no one is going to understand us no matter how hard we try. But if we do not open up about our grief, it's harder to realize how we are going to fix the damage, and our situation could end up getting worse. If you are having trouble opening up about or dealing with your grief, talking to a counselor may help. A good counselor will let you open up at your own pace without pressuring you, until sentence by sentence, word by word, it becomes easier to open up about your feelings. Not saying or doing anything about your grief will only make it more difficult. So if you feel like your friends won't understand, or you do not want to talk to a familiar face, go to a counselor. Tell them everything, the past, the present. If you feel like you are in depression and there is nothing you can do to make yourself feel better, talking to a grief therapist may be beneficial for you.

If over the course of time you feel like your condition is getting worse instead of showing improvement, you should see a doctor immediately. A mental health provider may help you identify the root cause and help you address your unresolved grief. As discussed previously, complicated grief can develop into depression and several other mental health issues. With help from a healthcare professional, it gets easier to reestablish your sense of control and return to your normal life gradually.

Grief Workshops & Art Therapy

There can be various ways through which you can help yourself feel good and ease your pain, two of which are grief workshops and art therapy. They benefit you by giving you a space to work through your grief.

Stress can grow over time when you forget to take good care of yourself. Life is unfair at many moments, and because of the constant disturbances that you are dealing with, you might forget to relax and take a break for a while. When it all becomes too much to deal with, you can always turn to art. Art can heal you in many forms.

The application of visual arts in terms of therapy is called art therapy. A therapist specializing in art therapy can help you creatively work through your grief. If you cannot imagine opening up about your pain and the concept of traditional therapy does not appeal to you, you may find it more appealing to work with an art therapist. An art therapist can gently help you open up through art and creative self-expression. Even if you don't want to see an art therapist, you can still benefit from the amazing therapeutic qualities of art. You can try several activities such as sculpting, creating collages, sketching, or painting. These activities can help you express and release your feelings when you just don't have the words.

Grief workshops are also a great option. When you feel like you are the only one hurting and grieving, you can always go to a grief workshop and feel welcomed by people who are in a similar situation. Some people find comfort in these workshops just by being around others who can better understand what they are going through.

Get Enough Sleep and Drink Water

This is something you have probably been hearing forever. Sleep helps to restore the energy that your body uses throughout the day. Every night, sleep helps your body to rest and recover. It helps you to heal. Moreover, it determines what to let go of and what to hold onto. During sleep, your brain develops pathways that allow you to navigate the coming day.

Furthermore, sleep helps to repair your heart and blood vessels. If you are not getting enough sleep, over time, you start to feel tired, overworked, and exhausted. You will also start to notice mood swings and will begin to feel sluggish.

According to a 2016 study, if you miss one hour of sleep, it will take up to four days to completely recover from it. (Gotter, 2019)

If you keep missing your sleep, you may develop a sleep deficit, which could lead to complications and symptoms of sleep deprivation. If you are having trouble sleeping, try listening to soothing music, releasing your feelings through art or journaling, or trying some of the meditations suggested in this book.

Drinking water is just as important as getting enough sleep and you should drink at least eight glasses of water daily to keep yourself hydrated and eliminate wastes from your body. Don't let yourself be dehydrated as it will further worsen your condition and slow down your healing process.

Write a Note Dedicated to Your Loss

If you are feeling restless and there are things that you wanted to say or share with the loved one you lost, or you want to tell someone about something you lost but you cannot speak about it yet, write your emotions, thoughts, and feelings in a note. Pen down whatever it is that is troubling you and throw it in a trash can. Doing so will help you open up about your loss and grief, and it will help you release the frustration, anger, and hurt you have been holding in for days, weeks, months, or even years. Writing down everything helps immensely. People who keep a journal will agree. The more you talk about your grief or pen it down, the lighter you will feel.

Chapter 5: When All You Can Do Is Laugh

My mom always had a great relationship with my husband; they had such fun and shared a great sense of humor. My mom was a very glamorous lady and used to joke with us to make sure she looked good when she died. When my mom passed away and was laid out in her coffin, her best friend provided clip-on earrings to complete my mom's glamorous look! However, when the time came to close the coffin, and we all had left the room, my mom's friend realized she never took the earrings back and asked my husband if he would retrieve them. My husband knew right then and there that my mom was having the last laugh.

Sometimes, grief can be treated with comedy, lots of it. The easiest way you can find to heal and come out of the darkness is by laughing hard. Here's a gentle reminder, it is okay to laugh when you are grieving. It can be useful therapy for you. Do not feel bad about finding things funny and laughing your lungs out about them. It can be just what your mind and body need for relaxation and getting you through bereavement.

You have every right to do what you feel comfortable with as you grieve a loss. Sometimes grieving can make us feel like we are going bonkers. We walk around in a fog and we forget things, make mistakes that seem silly, and have a hard time concentrating. It is so overwhelming. What better way to deal with it than to laugh at ourselves? Find humor in your mistakes and forgetfulness. It will remind you that what you are experiencing is normal, and it is okay.

Using humor as both a defense mechanism and coping tool during a time of grief helps a lot. After you face a huge loss and think you will no longer be able to laugh, it can be shocking to find yourself laughing at a random joke. You may wonder how on earth you can be laughing at a time like this. Please know that this reaction is completely normal. You don't have to think that you are going insane or something. You are normal if you use humor as a coping mechanism.

Keep in mind that healing asks for a dynamic approach, and if you rely on laughter following a loss, it never means that you don't still feel other emotions like being sad about what has just happened. Everyone needs to understand the fact that there is a time for everything; a time to cry, a time to remain serious and think about the shifts in your life, and a time to laugh. Keeping a healthy balance in your attitude will help you lead a balanced life.

Humor is a mature defense mechanism, just like defenses including forgiveness, tolerance, mindfulness, humility, and patience. Mature defense mechanisms help to motivate the development of feelings such as pleasure and control, and they are effective when it comes to helping a griever deal with complex and conflicting thoughts and emotions.

Of course, it is okay if you are unable to find something

that makes you laugh, which is why I have a few things you can consider:

Watch a Comedy Flick

This sounds as simple as it really is. Whenever you feel down, you can watch a comedy movie, maybe the one you have already watched ten times before, and laugh your lungs out. It can be fun to watch your favorite rom-com and enjoy the scenes that make you laugh and cry at the same time. Watching comedies is a perfect way to find a reason to laugh when your heart is only filled with grief and sorrow. No one is going to judge you. Be the captain of your ship, prepare the popcorn, and press play. Not just movies, you can also watch stand-up comedies and funny videos such as prank videos, pet videos, and other silly stuff that can help you feel refreshed and give you a good laugh. An hour spent laughing is better than a day spent crying. At least, this is what I believe. I hope this helps you too.

Read Funny Books

If you are an avid reader, you may find it easier to read some good funny books when you don't feel like talking to anyone. Funny books help you laugh out loud while remaining in your comfort zone. Good books can sometimes feel like your best friend, and if that friend is funny, you will definitely have a good time with them. If you don't have any favorites, you can always search online for recommendations of funny books that will make you laugh. Make your favorite coffee or tea, prepare some snacks, and enjoy your time with yourself.

Laugh At Yourself

When you are depressed and cannot find a reason to smile, learn to laugh at yourself. It will be very hard, and you will definitely feel stupid doing so, but believe me, laughing at yourself can be a great stress buster and healer.

This world appears to be divided into two groups of people; one group finds it easier to laugh at themselves when they fall or experience something embarrassing, while the other group deals with every situation a little more seriously. I feel those who fall and laugh hard are the ones with better health conditions. Being able to laugh at yourself is considered a healthy attitude and is known as a healthy attribute.

Laughter has various health benefits, as I discussed before. It aids in the release of endorphins as well as boosts your immune system.

A study conducted in 2019 by the University of Maryland Medical Center Baltimore's cardiologists showed that laughing combined with a good sense of humor protects against heart attack and reduces the chances of having heart disease. This study showed that people who had heart disease were 40% less likely to laugh in various situations than those of the same age but who had no heart disease.

Sign up for Funny Quotes

Here is how you can get another daily dose of laughter: you can subscribe to a source that sends daily funny quotes or stories to your phone number or email. That way, you don't have to make an effort to look for funny stuff to read online. Read them anytime during the day or at night when you are preparing to sleep and have a good laugh.

Tune Into Uplifting Podcasts

There is a long list of things that you can choose from when you want to find an escape in comedy and humor, and most of these things are quite easy. You do not have to do a lot, and you don't have to feel overwhelmed when doing these. They are meant to be easy and fun. Here is another one: listen to uplifting podcasts.

Listening to some positive words of powerful and influential people and even to those who have been or are going through the same things will be soothing and comforting. You will find the strength to confront your depression and grief and develop a positive attitude towards life and the days to come.

If you are not a fan of reading books or searching for quotes, you can use your sense of hearing and motivate yourself through inspiring stories of people who had it worse than you. It can help you to go easy on yourself and take inspiration from them. Sometimes, we do not realize how blessed we are even after losing someone or something important until we hear someone telling us how they lost things and people we still have in our lives.

Paint Your Toenails

This might sound funny but believe me, it works! Sometimes doing silly things can help us bring huge shifts in our moods and mental state. I know most of you would laugh at this and think, "How can painting your toenails be helpful?" Well, you can only know if you try. When the skies are grey and surrounded by negativity and darkness, bring in the colors. Paint your toenails a color completely outside your comfort zone; it's liberating! Use the colors you would never go for, challenge yourself. You will end up having a good laugh.

Float in the Air

Are you able to buy a hammock and use it? If so, you can either use it inside your house or outside. It is pure fun, and you will enjoy floating in the air for a while. Maybe you end up liking the idea so much that whenever you are sad, you will say, "It's hammock time." You can also install a swing if you have a backyard or a lawn. I would say do whatever it takes to make yourself comfortable and feel a little crazy. It won't hurt to act like a carefree child for a while. Your mind and body deserve it. It may bring you back to the days of your childhood when you used to enjoy riding the swing or see-saw. Embrace that feeling and allow it to comfort you.

Bring in a Pet

Are you a pet lover? Have you always wanted one? Maybe now is the time for you or a member of your family to adopt a pet. Pets can be a huge emotional support.

Research shows that interaction with animals can lead to increasing levels of the hormone called oxytocin. The hormone is also known as the bonding hormone, love hormone, or trust hormone. According to a study, making eye contact with dogs when you get home after work can lead to increased levels of oxytocin, as observed in women's samples. This hormone helps couples develop a strong sense of intimacy, and mothers develop a strong bond with their newborns. Moreover, oxytocin is linked to the development of strong trust and self-esteem. (Haley, 2015)

The interaction with a pet or any friendly animal not only increases oxytocin, but it can also increase levels of dopamine, a brain chemical that makes you feel good, and it can minimize levels of cortisol, the stress hormone. If you consider these benefits, you may want to bring a cute animal home as a pet and enjoy your time with it. Nowadays, various therapeutic interventions include interaction with animals, mainly because animals can help you cope with grief and cheer you up when you are feeling low.

So bring home a furry friend and remove your stress. Play with it, teach it tricks, and adore it loving you back the same way. Whatever you like, a cat, a dog, or a bird, a pet is a pet, and it will do its magic to make you feel happy.

Do What Makes You Happy

Pick something you absolutely love doing and do it. Make a date with yourself and make it happen. When you engage yourself in activities that make you feel better about yourself and your life, you are actually paving the way for yourself to get through this phase of darkness and cope with your loss. Enjoying your favorite activities can help you move towards accepting what is happening around you and dealing with what's happening within you.

Engage yourself in different activities. If you can, start a blog, or create a social media group for people who have been through the same or are still struggling. If you are an introvert, you can plan a movie night for yourself and if you feel like having company, invite a friend. Eat out if that makes you happy, or order your favorite food at home while watching a rom-com.

Do anything! No one is judging you. This is your time to relax and stay in your comfort zone. No one is going to push you out of it until you decide to come out and take on new challenges. If you like to sing, sing your heart out. If you love video games, grab that gaming console and begin. Remember, it is about you, and only you, so ask yourself, what makes you happy?

Wave at People

If you are out driving, wave enthusiastically at oncoming drivers and watch their reactions. This is hilarious and will really make you laugh. It is the small things that will work for you and make you feel better. You might have been thinking about big changes, but engaging yourself in small things like this that allow you to laugh or relax can also go a long way towards helping you heal. Waving at people might sound stupid to a lot of you, but if you give it a try, you will know what I am talking about.

While you grieve, you are taking out time for yourself. Your mind and body are at rest, so you have to ensure they get it. Some of these guidelines might have made you laugh already. So please know that doing these things can help make you happy and more comfortable.

Chapter 6: Self-Care is Self-Love

Love yourself first, and everything else falls in line. You really have to love yourself to get anything done in this world. – Lucille Ball

I have said this before, and I will say it again. Self-love is something you desperately need when you are grieving. Self-care is a way to show love to yourself. You need to ensure that you love and care for yourself at this time. When you appreciate yourself, your mind and body will respond positively. Just like I discussed the benefits of self-compassion earlier, and how it aids in your healing process, self-love and self-care are also powerful allies in the process.

Losing never comes easy. You have to deal with a lot in order to prepare yourself for the coming days and accept your reality as it is. Even if you saw it coming, it is still devastating when the moment arrives. You are unable to control yourself. Your mind and body no longer support you, and you end up messed up, broken, empty, and helpless. Watching someone you love die a tragic death can suck the peace and life out of you. The misery that this event put you through is unexplainable. I was in that situation some years ago, and I still cannot find the words to explain what it was like to lose my family one by one. Death comes with shock, grief, and disturbances and affects you like a hurricane, drifting you apart from your stability and patience. Grief is an emotion that requires self-expression, self-love, and self-compassion so that it becomes easier to cope with. However, it becomes easy to lose yourself in the chaos. It surely takes a toll on you while you don't even have the energy to fight. That's why self-care is so important.

Why Self-Care?

Self-care is a process through which we take care of our emotional, mental, and physical health. Though it may sound simple, it truly isn't easy, especially when times are hard, and you no longer know how you will get through the day, let alone consider your own well-being. We end up overlooking self-care when we are grieving after a major loss. We need to understand that good self-care will allow us to improve our moods and reduce anxiety. When you practice self-care, you make it possible to maintain a healthy relationship with yourself and other people.

Part of practicing self-care is ensuring you are getting enough sleep, adequate nutrition to maintain your well-being, and that you are engaging in physical exercise, so you remain fit and full of energy. Doing so will help your mind and body stay well and active.

Following a healthy routine can help you prepare for new challenges while you are grieving. In addition to that, you should also schedule weekly visits to your physician or therapist/counselor so that you can get all the external help you need to recover and heal.

Before you say, "It is not that easy," I want to add that grief surely is hard work, and it asks for a good amount of energy to be dealt with. It indeed exhausts you, making it difficult to do little things. For this reason, it is essential that we accept the fact that we might need some help from others, especially from our family and friends. Sometimes, we might need professional help, and we must accept that help instead of denying our mind and body's needs.

Nevertheless, I will never suggest you rush the process. Take your time in identifying a particular self-care routine that works for you as it is something you must actively plan. It is not something that happens on its own. You must treat it as an active choice and add all activities that you feel comfortable engaging in. It can also be fun to announce your plans to people you are close to so that you can feel a sense of commitment and motivation.

You should understand that it won't do the job if you don't see something you are doing as self-care. So you must be aware of the things you are doing as a part of your self-care routine. Tell yourself what you are doing, why you are doing it, and what outcome you expect from it.

Just remember one thing, whatever you are feeling, it is normal. Don't trap yourself in thinking about whether what you are feeling is right or wrong. Sadness, emptiness, confusion, fear, or whatever you feel, accept it instead of avoiding it. In the early stages of grief, emotions are raw, and you cannot understand what you feel. It is okay to go with the flow and let the dust settle.

What's Not Self-Care?

Knowing what is not self-care is essential. Something that we force ourselves to do or something that we dislike doing is never self-care. If a friend is forcing you to go to the gym with them or go out with them, and you are not ready for the 'going out' part, it is not self-care. Things that you are happy to engage in can fall under the label of self-care.

One major difference that you can spot between self-care and forced actions is that self-care is something that fills you with energy and improves your mood rather than exhausting you.

Some people think that self-care is just like being selfish when in reality, it is not. That is a lie that we tell ourselves because we feel like it would be unfair to the connection we just lost. If you feel like you are being unfair, tell yourself that your physical needs are important, especially if you are grieving a loss. If you think about the fact that practicing self-care helps you support your friends and family who are also coping with the loss, it helps you realize that self-care is not selfish at all.

Listen to your body, consider its needs. It will tell you when it is distressed and exhausted. If you feel this way, do not ignore it and let days pass by because grieving can cause serious physical suffering if you leave it unaddressed. The impact that a loss can create on your body can be serious. You can feel muscle pain and have trouble sleeping or eating. Sometimes you will wake up in the middle of the night and find yourself unable to sleep again. While grieving, your body asks for rest more than usual, so you must answer its call. Of course, your life will change after a loss, and so will your daily routine. It will take a little while to get back to your normal work routine, so be patient.

Your body is the house of your soul. You need to take care of it just like you take care of your own house. It, too, requires maintenance and care in order to protect you from unnecessary elements. The lethargy of grief is a term that most people use to define their sluggish state following a loss. It simply indicates that your body is asking you to slow down for a while and rest.

During this time, you can talk out whatever you are feeling. Talking out your grief can help you cope with it better. Voicing your feelings and thoughts can help the people around you understand your emotional and mental state. Also, opening up can give you some peace of mind. So try to express your grief as much as possible.

You have goals, and it can surely be tempting to march forward. However, after a loss, a person's mental state might not be too stable to make life-changing decisions, so it is better to wait for a while and not make any such decision that you may regret when you are healed. Some people choose to just move forward in order to avoid their pain. This is a mistake. Because if you make rash decisions and don't take your time to heal, you only complicate things further for yourself. Some common examples of making life-changing decisions are taking on new relationships, quitting jobs, etc. You may regret such changes later and feel bad about the choices you made when you were blinded by your grief.

You cannot run away from your suffering. It is a part of your journey. And only by going through it will you become a better and stronger version of yourself. So embrace whatever challenge life puts you through. We have to become our own saviors. Running away or finding a shortcut will only make it worse.

Grieving is an entirely personal process, and when you accept that there is no magic trick or secret formula to save you from suffering, you will be able to start your healing process. It will take as much time as it wants. But you can do things for yourself to make the process smoother and engage in things that make you happy and more comfortable in your skin. Be careful at every step, and I would suggest not burdening yourself with responsibilities that your body cannot handle. Flexibility is the key while you are grieving. If you are too rigid with what you are feeling and what you do about it, you will end up hurting yourself even more. So I would advise you to go with the flow and not create conflicts with your body and mind's natural reaction to your loss.

Every grief journey is different and unique, as is every individual griever who suffers, but one thing that all grievers have in common is the need for self-care.

Let's look into some smaller things that you can do right away to take care of yourself while you are grieving:

It's Okay to Say No Today

The first thing that I would ask you to focus on is to set boundaries. If you are a person who often doesn't say no to anything or anyone, you need to do it now. After a loss, it can be hard for you to manage things, and if people keep asking you to come out of your bubble and be more expressive about your feelings on top of that, don't hesitate to say no.

When you are going through something painful, your body needs relaxation, and for that, you need boundaries. You need to be more expressive about what you are willing to do and what you are not up for. These boundaries will protect your energy from being wasted on things you don't feel comfortable engaging in.

Learning to say no is absolutely fine. You don't have to feel bad about it or worry about how the other person will react. It is not your job to take care of everyone's emotions and feelings when you are grieving. Your job is to take care of yourself.

I will ask you not to shut yourself down and avoid interacting with people altogether, but I do encourage you to set boundaries. You deserve the space you are asking for. Don't let people force you into doing things that irritate you and interrupt your peace. Only you know how you can make it easier for yourself.

Take a Long Shower

Let the shower run a little longer today. Stay present as the water runs over you and soothes you. It can help you feel relaxed. You cannot completely alleviate the pain by taking long showers, but long showers can give you a good vibe, allowing you to diminish the pain.

With the water running over you, assume all the worries and pain are being washed away from your body. Close your eyes and feel as if your body is slowly releasing all the negative energy. It can sound funny, but when you are focused, you will see it actually works.

Taking a shower can help you clear your head. Of course, it is not a magic trick that would completely wash away all your sorrows and pain, but it helps relax your body and mind. When you walk out of the shower, you will surely feel relaxed and energized. So yes, taking long showers can help reduce the stress, even if it is just for a while.

Wear Comfortable Clothes

Wear soft clothes; when you are grieving, you want to feel your clothes are gentle and nonrestrictive. You don't have to dress up and make an appearance. Just pick out your most comfortable outfit and wear that after you take a long shower. Even if it is your favorite pajamas or shorts paired with a baggy sweatshirt, go with it. You are not following a dress code. Just remember my words; go easy on yourself. Wear whatever it is that makes you feel warm and cozy. Your comfort is all that matters. Being gentle and kind to your body is a favor that you must do for yourself. Don't neglect these little things because they play a part in your healing process. When you feel relaxed, you can rest well. It is not a lot—just small things. So pick out your favorite comfy clothes and treat your body well; give it the much-needed pampering it deserves.

Flowers Can Bring You Joy

No one can underestimate the healing power of flowers. From their smell to their fresh appearance, they hold the ability to make you feel refreshed and relaxed. Some flowers like lavender are also known for their therapeutic properties. When you are grieving, you can buy yourself flowers, soak in their beauty, and allow them to uplift you. This can be very refreshing and calming. It is one of the best self-care practices you can adopt to make yourself feel relaxed. Go to the nearest flower shop or order your favorite flowers online and place them all over your house or throw the petals in your hot bath water. Take a flower bath and let the fragrance calm your senses for hours. You can do it before sleep so as to get a good night's rest.

Let the Music Play

Put on your favorite song, and if you feel up to it, dance. I have found this to be a lifesaver. I might not feel like doing it at the time, but I have never finished dancing and regretted it. It's a huge mood booster.

You might have heard that music has the ability to evoke strong emotions. It also allows us to explore these emotions and live them fully while coming to peace with their existence. When you want to create a legitimate space for grieving, you can always turn to music. When we provide such space to our deepest emotions, it enables us to process and accept them as they are. People find music comforting when they are unable to find words to describe their pain. Music allows us to develop a connection with those who are also grieving.

In addition to that, when you wish to navigate your grief, music paves the way. It gives us the direction to discover our raw emotions. It allows us to identify our connection to grief and transform it into something valuable.

Music speaks to both mind and body. Through music, people have found ways to tell the world their stories, share their grief, and communicate what they feel. By putting our grief into music, we can give meaning to our deepest emotions and connect with others who are going through or have gone through the same situation.

When you want to calm yourself but still feel the existence of the connection that you just lost, you can do it through music. It helps you to explore the part of you that the person you loved and lost has left behind and enables you to rediscover that part of yourself.

Another thing that music helps us with is remembering. There may be a certain track that has some fond memories for you, or a song that reminds you of the loved one you have lost, and tuning into that can be comforting.

You can rely on music to help you grow stronger than your pain. It is surely a powerful tool that we can depend on during the hard times when we are in pain. So whenever you feel lost or out of words, you can find comfort in music. Play your favorite song and move your body. Feel the beats and let the lyrics help you connect with its rhythm. Allow it to help you while you navigate your grief and ease the healing process.

Go the Extra Mile

It may be breakfast; it may be midnight, have your favorite ice cream, open that pack of cookies,use the good dishes, turn the music up, sing out loud. Force yourself to lift your spirits. Do all the crazy stuff that you don't usually do. Go that extra mile just to make yourself feel comfortable and relaxed. Channel the energy of your emotions and find all the reasons to enjoy your own company. Redecorate your house, buy all the snacks you like. It is time to do the silly things, things that need a reason to happen. Give them the reason. Make your grief the reason to change the way you spend your days.

Doing extraordinary things will make your day more engaging. You will feel like you are changing, but the change is good because you do things that are NOT normal for you, and sometimes doing extraordinary things brings a refreshing change in your life and personality. Welcome that change and make it a part of your routine until you feel better about your situation. It is nice to accept a refreshing change when making peace with a drastic one. What matters is the fact that you are making an effort to accept the changes the loss has brought.

High-Five Yourself Every Now and Then

This may sound strange, but "high-five" yourself in the mirror every time you pass one. Cringeworthy as it may sound, this has given me a smile every time—little wins along the way. This can be a great way to make yourself feel appreciated. When words are no longer enough, and you need some motivation to get through the day, do this. You may also laugh at yourself while doing so, but this can be a healthy self-care practice. It can bring the motivation to move from one task to another, and gradually you will end up completing all the tasks on your to-do list. Silly as it may feel, it won't take a lot of effort. You can do it. You can appreciate yourself for being so strong and surviving the loss you are dealing with. Sometimes, when you feel proud of the effort you have put in, you end up feeling much more energized and motivated. I can assure you high-fives will help you with that.

Be Your Own Best Friend

It is time to become your own best friend. Buy a gorgeous candle that you would give to your best friend. Take it home, open it, light it, completely enjoy it, and thank yourself for being your own best friend today. Sounds easy, right? It will make you feel special and well-treated. You don't have to rely on others to treat you this way; you can be there for yourself and treat yourself the way you want to be treated. Of course, your friends and family can give you all the pampering during your suffering as well, but what you do for yourself has a unique effect on your mind and body.

It is not about abandoning your friends or avoiding interaction with anyone; it is only about being enough for yourself, even if it is just for a day. Tell yourself how important you are to yourself and that you are going to treat yourself better today than you have on other days.

Plan a Long Drive

Go for a drive if you can or have someone drive you, and enjoy the simple pleasure of travel. I love the open road, and when I am in the car alone, I love to listen to an audiobook. I could drive for miles. Hitting the road is the best option to give yourself some time out. I suggest you don't spend your days locked up in your room. Go out. Plan a long drive and leave all your worries behind. Watch the sunrise and sunset from the tallest building in your town or city. Dine out in your favorite restaurant and observe the beautiful views of nature. It will not only relax your body but also divert your mind for a while from overwhelming thoughts and emotions. Enjoy your peace while you travel in your car. Make no stops if you want; just keep going until you are homesick. It is not about avoiding your grief but giving yourself some space to navigate it while you let the wind brush across your skin and allow the peace to sink in.

Do What Brings You Closer to Your Loved Ones

Bake, cook, order in, do something you love that brings you comfort. Growing up, I loved when my mom baked rhubarb and custard crumble. No one in my own family likes it, but recently I baked it and ate it, and wow, did I feel like a kid again; it felt so comforting, and I felt closer to my mom. It's the little things!

You can do something else if it is not cooking that makes you feel closer to your loved one. It can be anything that makes you feel better and less anxious about what you are going to do with your life. This self-care guideline is only about connecting with the one you lost in some way so that you can remember the days when they were with you, and it will all feel much better this way.

Plan Ahead

Plan something to look forward to at a future date. This will help you to feel good and give you a sense of purpose. At the end of the day, when you are ready to sleep, say thanks to yourself for accomplishing the things you did today and outline goals for tomorrow. It can be simple tasks like grocery shopping, house cleaning, or anything. When you plan ahead, you go to sleep with high spirits and wake up motivated.

Keep in mind that we are not going to burden ourselves with a lot. Just a task or two would be enough. It just has to do the job and make you feel motivated to get out of your bed. Make it a habit; give yourself a purpose.

Chapter 7: Taking Care of Business

Acceptance in the mindful context means that even when the unthinkable happens, we honor ourselves and our experience with dignity and kindness. Rather than turn our back on our own suffering, we treat ourselves as we would a beloved friend. – Heather Stang

After a loss, it can often feel like practical matters are the furthest thing from our minds. When it is a struggle to get out of bed in the morning, the minutiae of day-to-day living can leave us feeling drained and overwhelmed.

It is easy to let day-to-day routines, housekeeping maintenance, and financial matters slip through the cracks. But over time, this can compound, turning minor annoyances into larger problems.

For this reason, it is important to be mindful of what your actions and reactions are leading you towards. Sometimes, we don't even realize how our choices, when grieving, can affect our future and day-to-day life. There are so many things that we may not want to deal with, but avoiding them can be a mistake because later on, they will just become even bigger and more difficult to deal with.

Rather than avoiding them, take a few minutes and think about how you can keep your finances and other practical matters under control. If even just the thought of it overwhelms you, go easy on yourself. Are there small steps you can take to help keep yourself on track?

Perhaps even just one small task a day can keep things from getting out of control.

Are there people that you can turn to for help? If keeping house is getting to you, is there a friend, family member, or significant other that wouldn't mind helping you keep up with it? Can you afford to hire a housekeeper? Be kind to yourself. Think of ways to unburden yourself with it while still keeping everything under control.

The same goes for financial matters. Do you know someone you trust who is good with numbers? Could they help you create a budget or keep track of expenses and payment due dates? If not, can you automate payments and set up auto reminders on your phone? The idea is to create a system that can keep things from slipping through the cracks. This gives you the space to grieve without that nagging feeling in the back of your mind about all the little things that you have been putting off that need to get done. The following guidelines are small things you can add to your system to keep your finances in order.

Check Your Balance Daily

Even if you are not spending a lot, make it a habit to check your bank balance daily. This is a small thing you can do to keep an eye on your finances, so you are prepared for what is to come. If you have more than one account, check all of them daily, and if you are currently using your money for any treatment or returning a loan, make sure you are left with enough money when you are done paying the required amount. Checking your bank balance daily will keep you well-informed and allow you to manage your expenses accordingly. It will help you catch little discrepancies before they become major problems.

Cancel Your Credit Cards

Another thing you can do to ease the burden of managing finances is to cancel your credit cards if at all possible. You have enough on your plate right now without worrying about missed payments and late fees. It is far too easy to let things slip a month or two here and there, and before you know it, the balance is out of control.

When I was going through a hard time, canceling my credit cards brought me a sense of relief. It was one less bill I had to manage, one less payment I had to worry about. Gone was the temptation to whip out the card and spend it on items I didn't need and couldn't afford.

If you are unable to cancel your credit card, instead of carrying it with you at all times, consider taking it out of your wallet or purse and keeping it in a safe place. That way, you will have access to it if you need it, but won't be faced with daily temptation. Little things like this can go a long way towards easing your mind about your day-to-day financial matters.

Sleep on a Purchasing Decision - Reduces Impulse Buying

Making small self-care purchases like some candles or a soft blanket are useful and can help you get through your grief. But some people use shopping as a coping mechanism. They feel like buying new stuff, even if it is irrelevant, will make them feel better. It is easy to give into those impulses and that can often lead to more problems. After that, they regret spending a lot on stuff they don't even need, and when their ruined finances stare back at them, they cry for help. If you are one of these people, you need to find a good solution so that you can stop spending unnecessarily.

Research has shown that emotions are responsible for people making shopping decisions. This is something that marketers all over the world know and use when they are working on advertisements or other kinds of promotional materials.

Retail therapy is a common coping mechanism that most people use. However, making impulsive decisions when it comes to shopping can lead to financial ruin. You must be sure to save your money or invest it so that you can get maximum return.

The main idea is not to say 'no' to yourself but to curb the habit of spending impulsively, which can gradually negatively impact your life.

Discuss Financial Matters with Your Financial Planner

It is a healthy habit to keep discussing your financial matters with an expert. You can hire one and rely on an expert's opinion when it comes to saving, spending, or investing your money. An expert can tell you how you should deal with things at the moment and how to prepare for future goals. Tell them your situation so that they can guide you properly and help you make well-informed decisions.

Discussing financial matters will allow you to be more goal-oriented and help you to stop spending aimlessly. It is an easy way to control your expenses and save your money.

Get Up to Speed on Any Insurance Policy

Do not ignore the updating of insurance policies. They are your saviors mainly at the time of need. I suggest you do not delay the task and get it done immediately. If you don't have insurance, I suggest you consider purchasing it. It offers financial security, so when you need medical help, you have it right away.

Plan a Budget

When you are grieving, managing finances can feel like a tough job, but don't let it scare you off. Take one step at a time. Calculate your daily, weekly, and monthly expenses and prepare a budget. In doing so, you will reduce your overspending and be able to meet your basic needs. You just have to begin taking charge, and the process will get easier along the way.

Planning a budget helps reduce stress and saves you from overwhelming responsibilities while you are coping with a loss. You never know when you will have to take out a huge sum of money from your savings. You are never prepared for a family emergency. Therefore, I suggest you keep things planned and refrain from spending on things that you have not included in your budget planning.

I was never prepared for family emergencies. It took me many years to heal. My financial situation became worse, and I lost so much. This is how I know that planning and budgeting are a must for every household. Learn to manage your finances and spend smartly. Even if you think you will never have such an emergency, plan for it anyway. Precaution is better than turning a blind eye. Life is always uncertain, and it often changes your situation just when you think you have everything under control.

Declutter Your House

One of the best things you can do when coping with grief is decluttering your house. Taking time out to do so can benefit you in many ways and can even be a part of your self-care routine. It can be such a relief to focus on things you have been avoiding for a long time—decluttering your house is one of them. Clean your house one day at a time, and you will see how much better you feel when you are done.

Take small sections and go for it. Start with your room if you like or with the attic. Choose the space where you want to begin and start cleaning. Take pleasure in finding things you thought you lost years ago, smile while looking at old photographs and gifts that your friends and family gave you. Celebrate little findings and make your days happier. It can not only help you clean and organize your house, but it can also give you purpose so you can be productive and active throughout the day, and the need to stay in bed all day and mourn will be minimized.

Check Up on Yourself

Set up a monthly reminder on your phone to check in with yourself and see how you are managing things. Self-care is important, as we discussed earlier. This is just another gentle reminder to tell you how important it is to keep checking up on yourself so you don't lose direction and can move forward as you heal and cope with your grief.

You can set up weekly and monthly reminders on your phone to ensure you are doing well and that your strategies to cope with grief are benefiting you. If no one checks up on you, tell yourself that you are enough and that you can check in with yourself on the progress you have made so far. Observe your patterns, see how far you have come and what's motivated you. Keep your spirits high. Don't let slow progress demotivate you. Whatever efforts you have made, commend yourself for your hard work and appreciate yourself for not breaking down during the process. Tell yourself that you have been a warrior, and your struggle will end one day.

Your weekly or monthly checkups will give you the motivation for the coming days. Practice self-appreciation, and you will feel just fine. A loss can shake your confidence, but you can build it back up through self-love and self-care. Don't look for a hero or a savior; become your own!

Chapter 8: Effective Meditations for Coping with Grief and Loss

Grief and loss are very important parts of our lives. Whether we have lived for 14 years or 40, we are bound to have experienced grief or loss in some form. When we find ourselves surrounded by such misfortunes, we receive all kinds of advice from others. Most people will tell you that it will pass and that you must not let it get to you.

However, that may be far from the truth. The only way to pull yourself from grief and loss is not by avoiding it but by going through it. Let yourself feel how you feel. Let yourself mourn the grievances that life has put you through. People do that in many different ways. Some talk about it, while others simply choose to cry without any words. One of the most appreciated ways of dealing with grief and loss is meditation.

Several techniques are available to help grievers in working through their grief. These can include counseling, be it one-on-one or in groups. Some people feel better after saying a prayer or a silent reflection, or communicating with nature.

Some types of meditation can benefit you more than others. If you have a practice for mindfulness, you already have a way to overcome your grief without worrying about how overwhelming it would be for you.

Your mindfulness will allow you to move through grief more productively, without worrying much about changes that are likely to come in life. Meditation teaches one thing clearly, i.e., everything can change.

Practicing mindfulness allows you to learn the art of letting go and enables you to overcome your grief so that you can focus on your feelings without rejecting or judging them. You will find a calming reassurance that exists between arising emotions, and slowly your mind begins to acknowledge them.

If you just faced a loss, you can find peace in some guided meditations that are designed for people going through the same situation. You only have to stop and listen with focus.

While there are a number of different meditations out there for you to try, not all are what you are looking for. This guide can help you narrow it down so you can find the meditation practice that is right for you.

Meditation 101

The concept of exercise and meditation is the same. There are several ways in which you can do both. You can go for a walk, go rock climbing, go swimming, or try Zumba. Also, you can meditate simply by taking a deep breath and focusing on the present. This helps you to develop a sense of gratitude.

Physical exercise gives strength to your body. Meditation is basically a mental exercise that gives strength to your brain. Another word for meditation is compassionate mind control.

When you are meditating, you are choosing the area where you want to divert your attention instead of just letting your mind wander in any direction. This is another way meditation is similar to exercise; it requires practice and training.

So if you have just started, know that you will get better with time. Do not get discouraged. It is not unusual for people who are new to meditation to think they are not good enough at it. Even if you feel like you are doing it wrong, do not give up trying.

According to my observation, there is no such thing as a good mediator or a bad meditator. There are just people who use meditation as a coping mechanism to recover and heal from their loss. When you begin controlling your mind, you will see effective and surprising results even if your attention keeps diverting during meditation.

If you are fully prepared to benefit from practicing meditation, you can start with guided meditation. In this meditation, a teacher is present to lead you, and you follow whatever they say and do. If you feel restless most of the time, you can benefit from meditation in motion, i.e., thai chi or yoga.

Here are the top six meditations that may work for you if you are dealing with grief and loss.

Focus & Concentration Meditation

When we are faced with any unfortunate event, we find our thoughts can be scattered all over the place. We often start thinking too much about a lot of different things. This puts our minds in an uncomfortable place and makes it hard for us to carry on with our day-to-day activities. As a result, tasks as simple as waking up and making coffee become inexplicably tough.

Such lack of focus and concentration is common in the early days of loss. In such times, practicing focus and concentration meditation could be extremely helpful. Focus and concentration meditations can be practiced in a number of ways. These can include very simple exercises such as closing your eyes and counting your breath. This not only breaks the chain of anxious thoughts but helps your body relax physically.

If you, too, feel like your thoughts are beginning to disturb your daily activities, or you find yourself unable to do anything without zoning out, or getting distracted by the thoughts of your unfortunate loss, here's what you need to do. Stop whatever you're doing at the moment.

Close your eyes and bring your focus to the blackness you see behind your eyes. Now take a deep breath in. Hold it for three seconds, and then slowly exhale. This counts as one breath. Repeat the deep breathing at least ten times, and count each one. As you breathe, make sure to keep the focus on how the air fills your lungs when you breathe in and hold it. Focus on how your chest heaves as you let it out. You can repeat the breathing process for as long as it takes for you to get rid of the thoughts that have been consuming your mind. The longer, the better.

One of the best things about this meditation is that it not only helps you mentally but also relieves you from a number of physical symptoms. While you deep breathe and focus on your breathing, your brain realizes that it is no longer in a fight or flight situation. The defensive mode of your body is shut down, and a lot of unconsciously tensed muscles are relaxed. It also relieves anxiety and frees you from worrisome thoughts that occupy your mind.

When you start practicing focusing and concentration meditation, you may find yourself struggling to actually focus on your breathing. Do not push yourself too hard since that would only stress you out and negate the effects of meditation. Just take more time and take more breaths. It may take a while, but sooner or later, you will be able to focus all your attention on your breathing and find yourself a lot calmer than before.

Mindfulness Meditation

When suffering from loss, it is very common for people to reflect excessively on the past where the loss didn't exist. On the contrary, others find themselves excessively worried about the future and what the loss would mean for it. However, while dealing with grief and loss, it is beneficial to allow ourselves to feel what we feel in the present moment without deflecting our feelings onto the past or future. This is where mindfulness meditation comes in.

Mindfulness can simply be defined as the ability to be completely and entirely present in the current moment and be aware of what one is doing and where one is. Mindfulness meditations are designed to help cultivate mindfulness in your nature, even if it is not a daily practice for you. Mindfulness meditations take time to bring about their effects. The first time you practice mindfulness meditation, you may not notice a great difference in how you feel. However, over the course of a few weeks or months, the change may become evident.

During mindfulness meditation, you may find yourself in a similar struggle as the focus and concentration meditation, but it won't go away just as easily. It may take days for you to be able to practice mindfulness in its true essence. But once you do, it will come to you very naturally and greatly impact how you deal with your grief and loss.

Mindfulness meditation can be practiced throughout the day in short spans. At any time, whether you are drifting off into the past or future or not, you can take a few moments to practice mindfulness. All you need to do is take note of your surroundings. Start from the bigger obvious things such as the people around you and what they're doing. Then move on to smaller details. Notice the feel and texture of the items you're holding or the surface you're sitting on—the temperature of the room and how it feels against your skin. Take in every detail of all that surrounds you.

Initially, no matter what you focus on, it will only enhance the feeling of grief and loss, but that is okay. Eventually, you will learn to appreciate the present moment rather than drifting off into a distant moment. Mindfulness helps you escape the thoughts of the past and future and makes you appreciate what you have in the present. Mindfulness reminds you that despite your losses in life, there is still a lot around you to be grateful for. It helps stop the negative and pessimistic thoughts that one might have following unfortunate events resulting in losses.

As mentioned earlier, mindfulness is best practiced throughout the day, every now and then. It helps you list more things that you still have in life and helps you stay grounded in the present whenever your mind wants to take you away into the past or future. A lot of people think that mindfulness means simply pretending that everything is okay, but that isn't what mindfulness is about. Mindfulness teaches you to be present in the current moment, be it a happy one or a sad one. It teaches you to allow yourself to actually feel the emotions that the present brings instead of avoiding them.When we worry about the past or future, we are avoiding our pain. When we practice mindfulness we are learning to sit with our pain and to be present with it, which is a far cry from simply pretending like everything is OK.

Compassion Meditation

Facing grief and loss can often leave us feeling very lonely. It often lands us in a pool of "Why me?" and makes us feel like we've been dealt very unfair cards in this game of life. The loneliness only leads to pessimism and misery that can become a permanent part of our life if we do not fight it. It can make anyone turn bitter to those around them and can negatively affect our relationships.

Compassion meditation can be very useful in the later stages of grief and loss, where we are trying to get back to our daily lives. Compassion meditations allow you to soften your heart. They help you realize that no matter how bad of a situation you are in, you are truly not alone in it. There are always people around you who may not share the same fortune but understand your feelings as you do theirs. Being compassionate makes it easier for you to accept those around you into your life and make you feel more connected to them. These meditations make you feel like you do not have to carry the weight of your loss alone.

When we find ourselves face to face with a loss or death that we didn't foresee, we find it hard to react to it in any way at all. At times like these, people around you will try to console and advise you on what you should do. While some people will express these sentiments carefully and thoughtfully, others may not. What are actually good intentions may come across as coercion or them trying to force you to have certain feelings. Developing bitter feelings towards these individuals can be very easy, even though all they are trying to do is help you out.

By practicing compassion meditation, you can help yourself understand how those around you probably have your best interest at heart. The suggestions you receive come from a place of concern and thoughtfulness, regardless of how they come across. You learn to understand and focus on how every person has their own struggles, and the advice they are giving you comes from a good place. They are most likely remembering how they dealt with their own struggles and offering you advice based on that. Even if their struggles are different from yours, they are struggles nevertheless, and we are all trying our best to get through them. Being able to understand this simple concept helps us be more open, loving, and kind to those around us. We perceive their words differently and do not take what they say personally.

Compassion meditation can be very helpful, but it is not recommended in the early phases of loss. When we lose someone, it is important that we focus on our loss, our emotions, and our grievances in order to face them completely. If practiced in the early phases, compassion meditation may lead individuals to ignore their own feelings and deflect them onto others. Therefore, it is important for us to face our emotions before we try to understand those of the others around us.

Sleeping Meditation

People dealing with grief and loss know that such events do not only disturb your mental health. You find yourself disturbed mentally as well as physically. While your heart and mind are consumed by grievance and mourning, your physical health is quite affected too. You may find yourself drained of all your energy and lethargic to a point where getting out of bed may seem like an impossible task. But regardless of how tired one feels, sometimes sleep seems to be out of the question.

Even years after one faces a loss, especially the death of a loved one, tossing and turning in bed remain constant. Sleep has been found to be one of the most affected routines in the lives of those who have gone through losses. But sleep is not something that can be compromised upon. Losing sleep, even for just a day, can really mess up our lives. So, losing sleep for days, months, and years is extremely detrimental to our physical and mental health.

Sleeping meditations are therefore very helpful for anyone who finds themselves restless at night, following a loss. These meditations help you relax and take your mind off the things that won't let you sleep. While it is very important to face the reality that you live in, if escaping for a little while helps you get some rest, I recommend embracing it wholeheartedly. Sleeping meditations are often guided meditations that guide you to relax your body. They help you unwind and loosen all your subconsciously tensed muscles. They also help paint an imaginary scenario where you can escape for a while and allow yourself to drift off into sleep.

Since sleeping problems and insomnia are common through all stages of grief, sleeping meditations are invaluable for years. They not only relieve your mind from constantly nagging thoughts that may be eating away at you but also help your body and mind finally get the rest that it deserves. It allows you to be better prepared for the coming day. When you wake up after a night of good sleep that sleeping meditation can help provide, you will find yourself having more energy to finally deal with your thoughts and do what you need to get done.

If you decide to make use of guided meditations, be aware beforehand that every guided meditation may not work for you. Guided meditations are of many different styles, and you may have to try many of them before you find one that works for you. So, if you are trying a guided sleep meditation, make sure you do not stress yourself if you still find yourself unable to sleep. And, unlike other meditations, sleeping meditations can go on for hours until you finally drift into a deep slumber. Try to stay relaxed and allow your body to take the time that it needs to relax enough to be able to sleep.

Meditation for Different Emotions

Grief and loss do not only bring sadness. Sometimes, they bring emotions that we do not anticipate and therefore do not understand. Being able to grieve your losses requires you to understand all the emotions that you are feeling and why you feel them. Sometimes we find anger and jealousy veiled as frustration and restlessness. And we often carry these emotions with us for a very long time. Because what we do not recognize, we cannot deal with. And what we do not deal with, we take with us.

These emotions end up being a burden that we have to take along with us and they weigh us down more than we realize. What starts out as an emotion starts impacting our physical health in the form of headaches and constant tiredness. We may experience more breakdowns and find it harder to accomplish tasks that previously did not take as much effort.

In order to pull ourselves out from such a phase, we can practice meditations for different emotions. Unlike some other meditations, these meditations do not help you concentrate on the outside world or those around you. Instead, they help you take a peek at yourself. They help you recognize and acknowledge what lies inside of you. These meditations take you through a wide range of emotions and help you understand them. While practicing these meditations, you may find yourself surprised by the emotions that you feel.

But that is not all that these meditations do. They also help you deal with these emotions. Knowing that you feel sad is not enough. You must know what to do with the sadness if you want to move on in life without the sadness weighing down on you. It is also important to understand that you may be feeling more than one emotion at once. You could be angry and regretful at the same time. Some losses bring people a bittersweet feeling that is often very hard to deal with. Practicing meditation for different emotions can help you acknowledge and accept these emotions so that you can deal with them in a better way.

Contemplative Meditation

Figuring out your life and your routines after a loss is a very important part of dealing with loss. Dealing with loss does not end with the emotions that you feel. It includes rehabilitating yourself and moving on with your daily routines. But people often find themselves stuck at this point.

When the losses are too great, people find themselves at a loss for thoughts of what to do next. It often seems impossible to be able to do anything anymore. This is common for people who find themselves jobless after losing a job that they had been doing for a very long period of time. Losing a job like that could leave them feeling purposeless and make them overlook everything that they could still do.

Contemplative meditation can prove to be helpful for such individuals as it would help them rebuild the life around them. Contemplative meditation helps one to keep an open mind and consider all their options. One may realize opportunities that they did not realize they had. Contemplative meditation does not force one to find answers, but it enables them to look at everything they are missing out on. This helps in piecing together solutions using one's own wisdom and truth.

Contemplation does not mean finding answers and solutions. On the contrary, it makes us ask questions. It makes us wonder about things that we have been avoiding and empowers us to then answer our own questions. Contemplative meditation not only helps us solve the problems that we see in front of us but also helps us identify hindrances that we do not see. It is an excellent way to pull ourselves through our grief, finding our own way, instead of taking one-size-fits-all pieces of advice.

Chapter 9: My Wish For You

"There are no happy endings. Endings are the saddest part, so just give me a happy middle and a very happy start." – Shel Silverstein, Every Thing On It

Firstly I would like to thank you for buying my book. I hope you are doing OK. None of us have chosen the losses we have experienced; we are forever left with unanswered questions and a hole in our heart that is never going away. I hope in some way these guidelines and meditations have been able to lift you, bring a smile to your face, and for a moment, help you along your journey.

As someone who has been through the same and grieved almost half of her life, I wish for you that you find the days get easier, you become stronger, and you keep going. Things might seem complicated right now but believe me when I say this; you have got this. It might sound cliché and unhelpful, but I know that you will find a purpose when you have healed and successfully overcome your loss. Once the skies are clear, you will see the sun.

One day, in the middle of the grieving process, you will wake up and decide that this is the day you get out of your bed and get back to life. You will see progress and determination in you that other people will admire. Let them wonder what brought you back or what gave you the motivation to be normal once again.

I know that grieving can take a lot of time, sometimes years, but I still wish for you to get your life's control back soon so that you don't end up regretting the years you passed doing nothing for yourself. These guidelines and meditations that I have shared with you are helpful for any form of loss. You can begin step by step and observe the change.

Losing a loved one is never easy. If you have been through something like that, I feel for you. I know things can take a toll on you when you are just trying to get through your days. However, I want you not just to live but to build yourself up and become an even better version of yourself. It took me years to get back on my feet, so I want to help you make your life easier.

The transition from acute grief to integrated grief is important, and in order to get there, it's important to embrace whatever you are feeling. Remember one thing; if you suppress your emotions, you will end up hurting yourself even more. Because the more you hide, the worse the outcome will be when your emotions explode one day like lava destroying every beautiful thing you have created over the years, be it business or relationships.

You bought my book because you wanted to heal, so whatever part of the world you belong to, I am happy to hear that you want to change your situation. I have said many times in the book that this process, healing, is never going to be easy. You have to provide yourself with all the help you can get.

You are not alone. You were never alone. I am here to support you, and there are thousands of people who understand how healing from a loss can take a toll on your health.

When your intention is great enough, you will ALWAYS find the time and energy to accomplish your desires. You can state excuses to the contrary, but holding on to your old stories is just another way of wasting precious time.
– James Arthur Ray

The most important aspect of healing and recovering from a loss is self-care and self-love. Once you learn to do that, you will be able to take the next step, which is taking care of your business, making financial plans, and getting back to your normal routine.

I will never ask you to push yourself to take the first step. However, I will surely tell you that you need to take this first step if you want to change your situation and heal. I wrote this book for people who have the power to improve themselves and become decision-makers, people who know that nothing is permanent and that losses will always leave us feeling empty. I learned that the hard way, so I wish you to learn it now, before realizing later that you could've done better for yourself.

I hope that you find healing and overcome your fears. Whatever loss you are dealing with, I hope that you find peace and comfort through this book. The things that I have mentioned in this book are the ones that I personally practiced and made a part of my routine after much trial and error. If only I had someone who had already been through it to show me the way! Not that I didn't know there could be guides out there to help me cope with my loss, but I was so absorbed in my grief that it took me years to come out of the dark and look for help. Now I want to become an example for people who share similar experiences.

When you are done reading this book, take a deep breath and say to yourself, "I am going to become a decision-maker and heal from the loss that has left me feeling empty. I will recover and help myself to focus on and appreciate what I have right now instead of worrying over and grieving what is gone."

I know you can do it. I believe in you because I did it. At times, I wondered if I would be able to survive after everything was gone, but here I am sharing my story and experiences with you. I am no hero but I am a survivor. I wish for you to become one as well and help others through your experiences.

I lost my family, house, and everything I held dear, but I am still standing. I wish for my readers to find the strength to open up about their loss, emotions, and feelings and accept their reality as it is.

The Cards You're Dealt was meant to make grieving easier for people because I had a hard time going through that process. I am looking forward to your reviews to see how my words and experiences have helped you cope with your grief. Please feel free to share in your review what part of my book inspired you the most.

I hope I was able to offer the help you needed. While writing this book, I remembered what it was like for me when I suffered huge losses and my life was upside down. This book holds my journey of pain and grief that I am sharing with you so you can do better. Good luck with your journey of coping with grief and loss.

Conclusion

"You gave me a forever within the numbered days..."

~ John Green, The Fault In Our Stars

Every day, thousands are born and thousands die. That is how life is, and that is how it was always meant to be. We may never even notice any of that until we experience a loss. In journeying through our pain, that is where we truly get to understand just how life is meant to be.

Behind the wide smiles, behind the strong exterior, there always lies a heart that is tender and soft. That is what makes us human. That is what connects us to the rest of the world. We cry, we laugh, we shed tears, we miss the dear ones that are no longer a part of our lives, only to realize that in some magical way, they are always there with us. They live in our memories, our mind, and our hearts. However, as comforting as that may sound, there are people who find it extremely hard to cope with grief.

No one can avoid loss as it is inevitable. We are going to lose people and things eventually. When we lose a connection that we have held dear, we grieve, and sometimes things get out of our control. Grieving a loss and coping with it requires strength and focus. However, both of these things can be difficult to expect from a griever.

Grieving is our body's natural way of regaining the rhythm of life. It is through grief that we let go of all that hurts us, and as everything in life, we too must eventually move on. As hard as that may sound, it is something that must be done.

When you are grieving, your life can become a black hole, but you need to stay strong and motivated. By taking the first step, you decide that you will heal from your loss and not spend your days lying in your bed, waiting for a miracle to happen that will change your situation.

When you begin, you can allow yourself to daydream and make yourself feel comforted with the things that remove mental and emotional pressure. Start with self-compassion, self-love, and self-appreciation. These things will create a strong base, and you will learn how to accept yourself along with all of your flaws. Some simple self-care tasks will bring you comfort when you are just starting, and it is all about going easy on yourself instead of feeling overwhelmed with a bunch of responsibilities.

Once you manage to get out of bed and engage yourself in small tasks, take the next step forward and enjoy the little things. Don't miss a moment to laugh and enjoy your time with your friends. Plan some things together, be it a movie or a simple meetup. Create chances to interact with people who make you feel loved and appreciated. And when the time comes, return the kindness received. Don't miss any chance to help the people who were there when you needed them the most.

Don't stop taking care of yourself; give yourself the space your mind and body require to relax. Develop a routine, start keeping a journal, engage your body in exercise so that you remain physically and mentally fit. If you need professional help, talk to a therapist. Also, there are ways to cope with your grief, such as grief workshops and art therapy; you can use them to aid in your healing process. Keep in mind that having enough sleep and drinking an adequate amount of water is necessary for your well-being. Sometimes, when things suddenly become a lot to deal with, write a note to the loved one you just lost. Say whatever it is you have been keeping in your heart.

If you use humor as a coping mechanism, be sure to have a good laugh at yourself. Find humor in silly jokes and do things that you never expected to see yourself doing such as waving at people, dancing crazily to your favorite song, painting your toenails in funky colors, reading funny books, and if you want to destress yourself, bring in a pet.

Some people think that engaging in self-care would be unfair to the connection they just lost. However, taking care of yourself simply means that you are appreciating your body for holding you for so long and supporting you without asking for too much. Self-care is not about going to fancy salons but wearing comfortable clothes, becoming your own best friend, eating what makes you happy, and going the extra mile for yourself just like you would do for your friends and family. Self-care is being mindful about what your mind and body are asking for and giving them the right treatment so you can stay healthy. You can also plan a long drive with your best friends. Another thing that can improve your mood and promote a healthy mental state is giving yourself a high-five whenever you see yourself in the mirror.

Taking care of your business is necessary not only for your present but also for your future. One must be prepared for days to come. When you are grieving, you might think that you have all the time in the world to take care of these things, while in reality, time is running out. So you need to act smartly and quickly. Things can get out of hand before you even know it.

You must not take any day for granted. Of course, you can take a rest and call it a day whenever you feel exhausted, but managing work or business is something you cannot keep ignoring for long.

If you need this book to make your healing process easier or know a friend or family member who might need it, buy this book for them, and help them figure out a way to crawl out of the darkness so that they can get back to life in time. Though grieving takes time, you should not let it consume you to the point that you lose the meaning of your existence and your life.

This book is a complete guide to help people who don't know where and how to begin. For the clueless and directionless, this book is a map. With the help of *The Cards You're Dealt*, begin navigating your grief and make peace with your reality. Please help yourself, so you don't regret your decisions later. Understand that losses are a part of living, and there will be several of them. We cannot undo something just because we don't like how it happened and when it happened. This is life, and it is never fair all the time.

Your strength must come from within. Find the courage to allow the pain inside, and then release it outside of you in time, so you don't end up hurt. Express as much as you can, and don't hide. The guilt should not be bigger than the need to fight and change. Allow your grief to find a home in you, but it is your job to learn to live with it. Remember, shutting yourself down will never be an option, even if you think it helps. It doesn't. So move on with a positive attitude and look forward to the coming days, so you are well prepared for the consequences following the loss.

We are all in this together. We all experience the ups and downs of life. The faces may be different, but rest assured, we all go through the same thing in one way or another. Grieving is a natural part of life, but it is one that can only serve a limited purpose. Dwelling in the past is neither healthy nor good for you or for those you love. It can not only cause you undue stress, but it can also have adverse effects on those around you. While the loss of a dear one is irreparable, the future life still remains to be lived. Live your life for those who would have wanted you to lead on in life, be happy and be successful. Live your life with gratitude, with friends, with a bit of laughter and joy because our time is always limited.

"Ain't no shame in holding on to grief... as long as you make room for other things too."

~ "Bubbles," The Wire

References

Angelo, Megan. (2013, August 6). *9 things Lucille Ball taught us about life.* Glamour. https://www.glamour.com/story/lucille-ball

Berrien, Elizabeth. (2013, July 2). *Creative grieving: A hip chick's path from loss to hope.* Greenleaf Book Group.

Geddes, L. (2018, October 23). *Why a daily bath helps beat depression – and how to have a good one.* The Guardian. https://www.theguardian.com/society/shortcuts/2018/oct/23/why-a-daily-bath-helps-beat-depression-and-how-to-have-a-good-one

Glock, Allison. (2015, April/May). *The G&G interview catching up with Bill Withers: Thirty years after walking away from music, Bill Withers joins the ranks of Rock and Roll Hall of Fame Royalty.* Garden & Gun. https://gardenandgun.com/articles/gg-interview-bill-withers/

Gotter, A. (2019, January 2). *Sleep Debt: Can You Ever Catch Up?* Healthline; Healthline Media. https://www.healthline.com/health/dr/sleep-deprivation/sleep-debt

Green, John.(2012, January 10). *The fault in our stars.* Dutton Books.

Haley, E. (2015, February 3). *The Healing Power of Animals.* Whats Your Grief. https://whatsyourgrief.com/healing-power-of-animals/

Life & death, a love story [Digital Image]. (2015). Retrieved from https://www.wattpad.com/story/51357426-life-death-a-love-story.

Magill, A. (2018, March 13). *What is the Relationship Between Food and Mood?* Mental Health First Aid. https://www.mentalhealthfirstaid.org/external/2018/03/relationship-food-mood/

Mayo Clinic Staff. (2019, August 24). *The health benefits of good friends.* Mayo Clinic. https://www.mayoclinic.org/healthy-lifestyle/adult-health/in-depth/friendships/art-20044860

Milne, A.A. (1996, October 1). *The Complete Tales of Winnie-the-Pooh.* Dutton Books for Young Readers.

Ray, A.J. (Writer). Siversten, L. (Collaborator). (2008). *Harmonic wealth: The secret of attracting the life you want.* Hyperion.

O'Donohue, John. (2008). *To bless the space between us: a book of blessings.* Doubleday.

Sahaja Online. (n.d.). *Coping with Loss & Grief.* Sahaja Online. https://sahajaonline.com/science-health/self-improvement-traits-abilities/loss-and-grief/

Silverstein, Shel. (2011, September 20). *Every thing on it.* HarperCollins.

Smith, L. (2018, May 16). *Can exercise help those dealing with grief?* Patient.info. https://patient.info/news-and-features/can-exercise-help-with-grief

Smith, M., Robinson, L., & Segal, J. (2020, September). *Coping with Grief and Loss.* HelpGuide.org. https://www.helpguide.org/articles/grief/coping-with-grief-and-loss.htm

Stang, Heather. (2014, March 1). *Mindfulness and grief: With guided meditations to calm your mind and restore your spiri*t.CICO books.

Strachan, G. (2019, August 19). *Caffeine and depression: Positive and negative effects.* MedicalNewsToday. https://www.medicalnewstoday.com/articles/313988#possible-benefits

Watson, K., & Potter, D. (2020, November 4). *10 Benefits of Drinking Hot Water.* Healthline. https://www.healthline.com/health/benefits-of-drinking-hot-water#reduces-stress

Williamson, K. (Writer), & Plec, Julie (Director). (2017, March 10). I was feeling epic. [Television series episode]. In Levy, B., Morgenstein, L., Plec, J. & Williamson K. (Creators). *The Vampire Diaries.* Warner Bros. Television Studios.

Zorzi, W.F. (Writer, story & teleplay), & Simon, D. (Writer, story), & Dickerson, E.(Director). (2008, January 13). Unconfirmed reports. [Television series episode]. In Simon, D. (Executive Producer), Noble, N. K. (Executive Producer), Thorson, K.L. (Producer), Chappelle, J. (Co-Executive Producer), & Burns, E. (Co-Executive Producer). *The Wire.* Blown Deadline Productions.

www.ingramcontent.com/pod-product-compliance
Lightning Source LLC
Chambersburg PA
CBHW052356060726
47592CB00020B/2450